The Evangelical Heritage

The Evangelical Heritage

A Study in Historical Theology

Bernard Ramm
Foreword by Kevin Vanhoozer

Baker Books
A Division of Baker Book House Co
Grand Rapids, Michigan 49516

Reprinted 1981, 2000 by Baker Books
a division of Baker Book House Company
P.O. Box 6287, Grand Rapids, MI 49516-6287
with permission of copyright holder

Foreword ©2000 by Baker Book House Company

Printed in the United States of America

Library of Congress Cataloging-in-Publication Data

Ramm, Bernard L., 1916–1992
    The evangelical heritage : a study in historical theology / Bernard Ramm ; introduction by Kevin Vanhoozer.
        p.   cm.
    Originally published: Waco, Tex. : Word Books, 1973.
    Includes bibliographical references and index.
      ISBN: 0-8010-2238-X (pbk : alk. paper)
      Evangelicalism—History. I. Title.
    BR1640.R35 2000
    230'.04624'09—dc21   00-030399

For information about academic books, resources for Christian leaders, and all new releases available from Baker Book House, visit our web site:
http://www.bakerbooks.com

With eternal gratitude to my brother,
John Bernard Ramm,
who was the human instrument in leading me
to hear the words of eternal life whereupon believing
them all things became new.

CONTENTS

THE PATTERN OF EVANGELICAL THEOLOGY: HOMMAGE À RAMM

Kevin J. Vanhoozer
Research Professor of Systematic Theology
The Divinity School
Trinity International University

Between the times: introducing Bernard Ramm

Once, after he had just finished hearing Bernard Ramm lecture on evangelical theology, a shrewd listener asked Ramm to define American evangelical theology more precisely. Ramm reports having experienced inward panic as he realized that this was his nightmare question: "Like a drowning man who sees parts of his life pass before him at great speed . . . so my theology passed before my eyes. I saw my theology as a series of doctrines picked up here and there, like a rag-bag collection."[1] Even Ramm was not satisfied with the answer he stuttered out in reply. Upon further reflection, Ramm came to see that his theology was the product of the struggle between orthodox and liberal theology that has dominated the twentieth-century discussion. This debate and the fundamentalist-modernist controversy that was at the eye of the storm have, in Ramm's words, "warped" evangelical theology.

As we enter the twenty-first century, Ramm's nightmare question threatens to become a living nightmare as various factions struggle both to define and to possess the soul of evangelical theology. Ramm is, of course, no longer a part of the debate; he died in

1992. Yet he was instrumental in forging evangelical theology through his early textbooks on apologetics and hermeneutics, and his later work was largely devoted to articulating its inner structure. *The Evangelical Heritage* is as relevant today as it was when first published in 1973, perhaps even more so. For in this work Ramm approaches the question of the identity of evangelical theology against a long and large historical backdrop. This was his way of resisting the temptation to define evangelical theology by way of contrast with its immediate opponents. Accordingly, Ramm's *Evangelical Heritage* may be viewed as a heroic attempt to repair the warp.

The best and worst of evangelical times

Ramm worked between the times—between the emergence of evangelical theology from fundamentalism on the one hand and its more recent encounter with postliberalism on the other—a period which was both the best and worst of times for evangelical theology.

It was the best of times. After the Second World War evangelical theologians established their distinct identity over against fundamentalists on the grounds that they would engage with the best of secular scholarship rather than keep it at arm's length. The 1940s and 1950s saw the emergence of new institutions such as the National Association of Evangelicals and *Christianity Today*. By the mid 1970s, *Time* magazine had announced the year of the evangelical. And in the late 1980s and 1990s, modern liberal theology was on the retreat, due in large part to the rise of postmodernity. With the demise of the assumption that knowledge arose from *pure reason*, and with the acknowledgment that all knowing begins in some kind of faith, evangelicals found themselves as respectable, epistemologically speaking, as any other tradition. Evangelical theology was given the intellectual equivalent of a seat on the United Nations Security Council. At last, seated comfortably at the table, evangelical theology had arrived.

It was the worst of times. There are those who lament that, having been seated at the table, evangelicals had nothing to say. Mark Noll has decried the scandal of the evangelical mind;[2] David Wells concurred, arguing that there was "no place for truth" in evangelical theology, preoccupied as it was with popular culture and pious experience.[3] There are confusions about the distinctiveness of evangelical theology vis-à-vis fundamentalism on the one hand, and postliberalism on the other.[4] Evangelicals themselves are divided over the question of theological identity and theological integrity, and book-length statements of affirmations and essentials have not yet solved the identity crisis. Nor is the problem confined to North America alone.[5]

Behind or ahead of the times?

In the midst of divisions and diversity, Ramm invites us to take the long historical view, to stand back from our present controversies in order to remind ourselves where we have come from and upon whose shoulders we are standing. He is not indifferent to new challenges, as the last two chapters make abundantly clear, yet at the same time he insists that there is indeed a heritage from which to begin our search for self-understanding.

Evangelical theology is not the only discipline that looks back to its heritage. Consider, for instance, French composer Claude Debussy's piano composition "Hommage à Rameau," part of his *Images* (1905–7). Jean-Philippe Rameau was himself an eighteenth-century composer and theorist who sought to adhere to principles that were in line with the rationalist outlook of his times. Debussy's composition pays homage to the past while simultaneously working in a distinctly new musical idiom, impressionism.

Ramm, similarly, is conscious of his obligation to past theologians. Yet he is also aware, as was Debussy, of the new cultural and intellectual idioms of the twentieth-century. Unlike Debussy, however, Ramm's interest in the evangelical heritage centers not on questions of style, but rather on questions of substance and structure. *The riddle of evangelical identity is precisely the problem of how to preserve the structure and substance of the evangelical heritage in a new, post-Enlightenment, situation.*

The title of the present work—*The Evangelical Heritage*—may lead some readers to think that the book is primarily about the past. That would be a perfunctory reading. On the contrary, in deciding to reclaim the heritage in order to address present problems of evangelical identity, Ramm was actually ahead of his time. For though Ramm never uses the term *postmodern*, this was the kind of evangelical theology towards which he was working, if one takes *postmodern* in the sense of "beyond or after modernity." *The Evangelical Heritage* moves between the times: Ramm roots evangelical

theology in premodern times, confronts evangelical thought with the
theology of modernity, and explores a way of doing theology that
could be labelled postmodern which would nevertheless preserve
the evangelical heritage. In particular, Ramm anticipates in this work
aspects of three different varieties of *postmodern orthodoxy.*

Paleo-orthodoxy. Thomas Oden advocates a paleo-orthodoxy in
which Christians today read the Bible with the church fathers.[6]
One of the benefits of the critique of modernity's myth of *universal reason* has been a recovery of the richness of particular traditions. Oden believes that liberal theology, precisely because it
sought correlations with contemporary culture, will not outlast the
death of modernity. What must guide the church in our after-
modern times, Oden believes, is the consensus of the ancient and
premodern church about the meaning of Scripture. To this end, he
has spearheaded an ambitious publishing campaign to make available the best of patristic commentary on every book of the Bible.[7]
Ramm would surely have welcomed such an initiative, given his
understanding of theology as a form of biblical interpretation and
his emphasis on the evangelical heritage. Indeed, Ramm early on
defined evangelicalism as "the historic Christian faith as reflected
in the great creeds of the ancient Church, and in the spirit and writings of the Reformers."[8]

Radical orthodoxy. Quite another response to modernity may be
seen in the work of a group of Cambridge theologians centered
around John Milbank.[9] Radical Orthodoxy is a blast against *secular reason,* against the attempt to think about the world and about
human beings non-theologically. Like the paleo-orthodox, Milbank
believes that creedal Christianity needs to be recovered, but he goes
further by insisting that the great doctrines of the Incarnation and
Trinity become the framework for thinking about the world and
everything in the world. Ramm would agree at least this far: that it
is unwise to cede the realm of scientific truth, or any other kind of
truth for that matter, to secularity. He opposed obscurantism, that
is, the denial of modern learning. At the same time, Ramm saw
clearly that "the root of humanism must be religion, for humanism
could not sustain itself."[10] Evangelical theology should not be
opposed either to culture or to humanism; rather, it should seek to
reclaim both. In Ramm's words, "In essence evangelical theology is
not anticultural, world-denying."[11]

Neo-orthodoxy. A number of recent studies have suggested that Karl Barth was actually a postmodern theologian, perhaps even the prototype postmodern theologian.[12] One of the reasons Ramm was attracted to Barth is precisely because of his critique of modern liberal theology. Ramm leaves us in no doubt as to his general admiration for Barth's theology, going so far in 1983, with the publication of *After Fundamentalism*, as to commend Barth's theology as the best model yet for evangelical theology. I shall return to the question of Ramm's "Barthian" streak in due course. My present concern is to draw attention to the many ways in which Ramm's writings on evangelical theology could be construed as an attempt to preserve the heritage in a postmodern age. Ramm consequently shows himself, in this book and in others, to be a thinker of the avant-garde, not the rear guard.

A house divided against itself? Ramm among the theologians

> "A house divided against itself cannot stand."
> Matthew 12:25

"Mere evangelicalism"

Internecine warfare about non-essentials is the bane of evangelical existence. This may be the true scandal of the evangelical mind, for as Ramm notes, it is most typical of cults to major on the minors. Evangelicals are sometimes prone to doing so as well—it is another symptom of the "warp"—and Ramm mentions the emphasis on eschatology as a case in point.[13] Such cult-like behavior is the consequence, he believes, of the failure to grasp the "inner structure" or "pattern" of evangelical theology. Furthermore, the failure to discern the inner structure of evangelical theology is precisely what leads to Ramm's nightmare question and the concomitant inability to articulate the unity in which evangelical theology exists.

Evangelical has become an essentially disputed concept. Ramm is not the only one to worry that the next generation of evangelicals will inherit a divided house, a legacy of bickering and fragmentation. The break-up of evangelical theology would mean the heritage had been squandered. "I am of Henry"; "I belong to Ramm"; "I belong to Bloesch." All three of these theologians would doubtless reject such factionalism. What is more important is that

"I belong to Christ," all the more so because every theologian, no matter how gifted, is both saint and sinner, finite and fallen. *The Evangelical Heritage* is therefore not a tract for a Rammian school of theology. Readers wishing to join a new theological party will likely be disappointed. Ramm does not always give us his own thinking on several crucial issues (e.g., the openness of God). No, the strength of the book lies elsewhere, in its call for a return to what we might term "mere evangelicalism." This is not simply a return to a generic "mere Christianity" that affirms the great creeds; mere evangelicalism should not be confused with paleo-orthodoxy. No, Ramm believes that evangelical theology, while clearly creedal, nevertheless displays a structure and spirit—a "mereness"—all its own. He arrives at mere evangelicalism by holding fast to "whatever is true . . . whatever is right" (Phil. 4:8)—to whatever corresponds to and upholds the evangel—in the history of theology. What emerges in the following pages, then, is not a third-person history of theology, but an account of the rock from which we were hewn, a story aimed at fostering greater evangelical self-understanding.

Ramm's attempt to derive mere evangelicalism from the history of theology enables him to confront the root-problem concerning the unity of evangelical theology in a constructive and compelling manner. For by locating mere evangelicalism in the history of theology, Ramm is finally able to define the movement *other than* by reference to the modernist-fundamentalist controversy. Obviously, evangelical theology has to respond to the project of modernity; yet it does not follow that evangelical theology need *define* itself in opposition to the project of modernity.

Ramm's *The Evangelical Heritage* thus leads the reader in a slightly different direction than that of J. Gresham Machen's celebrated *Christianity and Liberalism*.[14] Machen was concerned to distance genuine Christian faith from its modern counterpart in order to preserve the integrity of the gospel message. Ramm critically engages with liberalism too, and for the same reason. Yet Ramm's work also raises another question, one that probably was not even a blip on Machen's radar screen. It concerns the extent to which mid–twentieth-century evangelicalism might itself be inadvertently modern in its method. The question is this: has evangelical theology related to modernity according to Newton's third law of motion, "For every action there is an equal and opposite reaction"? For example, have modern critical doubts about the Bible—questions of authorship and historicity—prompted an "equal and opposite" emphasis on authorship and historicity by evangelicals? Ramm's worry about evangelical theology being warped by the fundamentalist-modernist debate takes on new urgency. Incidentally, I believe that it was precisely because Barth attempted to respond (not react!) to the Enlightenment with properly theological resources (e.g., Christology) that Ramm in his later years felt an increasing attraction to his theology.[15]

The splintered spectrum: right, left, or center?

Some years back Lonnie Kliever wrote a survey of contemporary theology titled *The Shattered Spectrum*. If anything, the spectrum is even more fragmented today. Even within the evangelical fragment of this spectrum, several splinters may be distinguished. Where does Ramm fit into the evangelical spectrum of theology?

According to Clark Pinnock's threefold typology of (1) "progressives" who revise the biblical text in light of the present context, (2) "conservatives" who privilege the biblical text and resist the present context, and (3) "moderates" who see the importance of both text and present context, it is clear that Ramm, like many evangelicals, would be a moderate.[16]

On Millard Erickson's reading, on the other hand, Ramm belongs with other "postconservatives" on the "evangelical left."[17] While Ramm does indeed share with others on the left a concern about how to respond to the Enlightenment, he does not hold to all the points that Erickson, following Roger Olson, lists as characteristic of left-wing theologians.[18] It would be very difficult to document from Ramm's writing his agreement with more than half of these points. Erickson's main reason, I believe, for placing Ramm on the left is because of his (guilty?) association with Karl Barth. Erickson is especially troubled by Ramm's ambiguity in *After Fundamentalism* when it comes to just how Barth's theology represents a paradigmatic "method" for evangelicals.

Erickson's ambivalence is warranted, at least in part. It is not entirely clear from *After Fundamentalism* just how Barth could serve as a new paradigm for evangelical theological method. What does come through is Ramm's conviction that Barth somehow was able to engage the Enlightenment without capitulating to it. On Ramm's reading, Barth neither caves in to nor flees from modernity. The key litmus test is Barth's doctrine of Scripture, together with his biblical exegesis.

Ramm felt that Barth had recovered something of the deep structure, though not the entire blueprint, of evangelical theological method. He argued that Barth had correctly preserved, in a post-Enlightenment idiom, the notion that revelation is a matter of Word *and* Spirit: "the Spirit speaking in the Scriptures." This fuller version of divine revelation was what had earlier attracted Ramm to the Reformers. Conservative evangelicalism, Ramm feared, was in danger of lapsing, not towards legalism like the Galatians, but towards "letterism" like the fundamentalists.[19]

Ramm's ultimate allegiance lay with the orthodox heritage, particularly as interpreted by the Reformers. I think Ramm worried that evangelicalism might fall prey to what he called an "abbreviated Protestant principle" that recognizes the authority of Word but not of Spirit. Further, I think that Ramm saw in Barth a recovery of the Reformation principle of "the Spirit speaking in the Scriptures." However, Ramm's attempt to mediate between conservative evangelical and Barthian theology lacked the conceptual resources necessary for successful communication, much less reconciliation.[20]

Erickson does not mention one of Ramm's significant later statements about Barth, expressed in the brief article "Helps from Karl Barth," which was part of a volume celebrating the centenary of Barth's birth.[21] In that article, Ramm mentions three ways in which Barth helped him as an evangelical theologian. First, Ramm learned from Barth that theology should proceed from a full faith in the truth of God and not fear anything that unbelieving intellectuals (or biblical critics) might throw in one's path. In brief, one did not first have to build one's faith on the basis of sufficient evidence.[22] The second material impact of Barth's theology on Ramm's thought lay in the respect it inculcated for historical theology. Church theology, Barth thought, must be in "ecumenical" discussion with the theologians who have gone before. In this sense, we can thank Barth for his part in inspiring Ramm to write *The Evangelical Heritage*.

Lastly, Ramm credits Barth for showing him how to correlate the critical study of Scripture (its "humanity") with theological interpretation (its "divinity"). It is not the "letter" of the text but the "Spirit of the letter" that conveys the Word of God. Yet Ramm remains uneasy. He concludes his article with the thought that Barth "is not home free." Barth points in a direction, but his theology is not itself the evangelicals' theological promised land. Thus Ramm's final comment: "We hope that in the future someone will put Barth's thesis together in a more convincing way . . . [then] we shall know better how to correlate biblical criticism, divine revelation, divine inspiration, divine authority of Scripture, and its place as the Word of God in the church."[23] While it may be fair to say that Ramm had leftward leanings, it should not be forgotten that his feet were planted in the center.

Protestant and Christocentric: the structure of Ramm's mature theological thought

There is little point in trying to defend Ramm's theological judgment at every point. It is possible that the very fundamentalist-liberal controversy that gave rise to evangelicalism warped Ramm's thinking at certain points as well. What is worth defending, in my view, is the theological soundness and value of his vision for what I am calling "mere evangelicalism." Evangelicalism must be distinct from both fundamentalism and liberalism alike. In Ramm's retelling of the story of evangelical theology it was modernity, ironically enough, that begat fundamentalism.

The Ramm I admire is the Ramm who authored an important trilogy that could be taken (almost!) as laying out the theological method for mere evangelicalism. The books are *The Pattern of Religious Authority* (1957), *The Witness of the Spirit* (1959), and *Special Revelation and the Word of God* (1961). These three books, together with *Protestant Biblical Interpretation* (3rd ed., 1970) and *The Evangelical Heritage*, comprise that part of Ramm's corpus which I believe to be of continuing value. To repeat: what is most valuable in Ramm's writings is his sense, not always fully articulated, of mere evangelicalism, his emphasis on the need to grasp the inner structure of evangelical theology. It is possible to sum up the inner structure of Ramm's own theology under two major headings: the "Protestant principle" and the "Christocentric principle."

The Protestant principle

The Protestant principle has to do with the locus of religious authority. Who speaks for God? Where can we find God's say-so? For Protestants, says Ramm, authority is located not in the institutional church, nor in the best human philosophies, nor in individual experience, but rather in the Scriptures. To be precise, the Protes-

tant principle maintains that God's authority is to be identified with
"the Holy Spirit speaking in the Scripture" (*Westminster Confession
of Faith* I.x). The authentic, full-blown Protestant principle recognizes both an objective revelation (the Spirit-inspired Scripture) and
a subjective divine witness (the Spirit-illumined Scripture).

The *abbreviated* Protestant principle, in contrast, states that the
Bible, and the Bible alone (e.g., *sans* Spirit), is authoritative. In
Ramm's opinion, such a view falsifies the structure of theological
authority by omitting the internal testimony of the Spirit. One reason for this neglect of the active role of the Spirit is, once again,
the polemical context out of which evangelicalism emerged. Ramm
states that "fundamentalism was so concerned to defend the inspiration of the Scriptures against all liberals outside the camp . . . that
it lost track of the more comprehensive doctrine of revelation."[24]
The truer Protestant principle, says Ramm, is that "there is an *external* principle (the *inspired* Scripture) and an *internal* principle (the
witness of the Holy Spirit)."[25] The proper principle of authority in
the Christian church is "the Holy Spirit speaking in the Scriptures."[26] The Scriptures themselves are the product of the Spirit's
inspiration. Ramm agrees with Luther that the Spirit never contra-
dicts himself; on the contrary, the Spirit seals the written word on
the hearts and minds of the reader. This is also why Ramm suggests
that the dichotomy—either revelation is propositional or it is non-
propositional—is misleading and unhelpful.

We may now return to Erickson's judgment that Ramm belongs
on the evangelical left. In Erickson's words, "It is apparent . . . that
a shift toward a more ambiguous relationship between revelation
and the words of Scripture has taken place in Ramm's view of Scripture."[27] Does Ramm indeed affirm Barth's distinction between the
Word of God and Scripture (Ramm calls it a *diastis* or "interval")?

It is very likely that Ramm saw Barth as affirming, or at least
coming quite close to affirming, the genuine Protestant principle.
For it is possible to read Barth's remarks about the Bible "becoming" the Word of God in terms of Ramm's dual insistence on revelation involving both the objective Word and the subjective testimony of the Spirit ("the Spirit speaking in the Scriptures"). Ramm
believes himself to be siding with the Reformers in his reluctance
to identify the Bible with the Word of God apart from the internal
witness of the Holy Spirit.[28] This reticence stems not from a dis-
belief in propositional revelation but rather from a conviction that

revelation, while cognitive and informative, is also *more* than merely informative. Ramm notes that the Bible, through literary forms such as poetry, song, parable, and apocalyptic, appeals to the imagination as well as to the mind.[29]

Despite his reservations with the idea that revelation is *solely* propositional, it would be wrong to identify Ramm with those who hold a non-propositional view of revelation. Indeed, Ramm himself notes that those who identify Jesus Christ alone as the Word of God are still able to write lengthy textbooks in theology! He pointedly observes, "No theologian can perform the miracle of deriving conceptual elements from a revelation that is purely nonconceptual, that is, the pure presence of God."[30] On the other hand, revelation is not simply a set of propositions, but a personal presence: "It is something spiritual as well as rational; it is confrontation as well as speaking."[31] If one reads widely enough in post-Reformation Protestant theology, Ramm pointedly notes, one will discover a number of "pre–neo-orthodox" theologians who view revelation in terms of the divine presence as much as in terms of the divine disclosure of truth.[32] Ramm's Protestant principle is best seen as an attempt to recover, not to modify, the evangelical heritage concerning biblical authority.

The Christocentric principle

The "Word and Spirit" principle at the heart of Reformation Protestantism is neither purely formal nor arbitrary. The Protestant principle alone does not, therefore, represent the final word on the subject of religious authority. Ramm's view concerning the inner structure of evangelical theology would be incomplete if we failed to consider what he regarded as its foundation: the person and work of Jesus Christ.

Jesus Christ—true God become true man—is the substance of revelation, the reality to which both Word and Spirit witness. The danger of abbreviated Protestantism rears its ugly head here too: "The temptation of biblicism is that it can speak of the inspiration of the Scriptures *apart from* the Lord they enshrine."[33] In other words, the Protestant principle is not an end in itself. Yes, authority lies with "the Spirit speaking in the Scriptures." But this is not the end of the story. We must go on to specify just what the Spirit is saying in the Scriptures. For the whole point of having an authoritative Scripture is to hear the gospel message of Jesus Christ, the salvation of God for sinners.

Interestingly enough, Ramm draws a sharp contrast between his own position and that of Barth precisely at the point where one might have thought there would be the greatest commonality, namely, in Christology. Ramm observes, "A Christocentrist believes that Christ is the center of Scripture, the center of theology, and the center of the gospel. I am a Christocentrist. But Christomonism is Christocentrism carried to the extreme . . . Barth is a Christomonist."[34]

What does Christocentrism mean? Here is Ramm's answer, a brief Christocentric manifesto:

> Christ is the supreme object of the witness of the Spirit, and Christ is the supreme content of the Scriptures. The Scriptures are inspired by the Spirit and they witness supremely to Christ, the personal Word of God. Such is the pattern of authority, and the three elements of it must be held in proper relationship. The cultist [with whom Ramm is comparing the fundamentalist] fails to keep the person and work of Jesus Christ central."[35]

So here we have the structure of Ramm's thought, and his prescription for evangelical theology. Revelation lies at the center of evangelical theology, Scripture and Spirit at the center of the doctrine of revelation, and Christ at the center of the Scripture's and the Spirit's witness.

The integrity of evangelical theology: the science of God's word-act

What is ultimately at stake in today's debates concerning the nature of evangelicalism is the theological integrity of the movement. If evangelical theology is to be different from the discredited science of phrenology or the pseudo-science of astrology, it must have a real subject matter and an adequate method for gaining knowledge of it.

What, then, is the distinct subject matter of theology? It follows from the two principles we have examined above that the fundamental datum of evangelical theology is the act-and-word of God. *Evangelical theology is essentially the interpretation of the gospel of Jesus Christ as rendered in history and in Scripture.* In Ramm's words, "Evangelical Christianity refers to that version of Christianity which places the priority of the Word and Act of God over the faith, response, or experiences of men. Concretely this means the supremacy and authority of the Word of God (as a synonym for all the revelation of God, written and unwritten) over all human philosophies or religions."[36]

Evangelical theology thus begins with God's self-giving. Ramm rightly insists that this self-giving involves God's act-and-word. Revelation is neither a monism of the act (as in the Biblical Theology Movement of the 1950s) nor a monism of the word (the temptation of Fundamentalism, in Ramm's view). Rather, the written word has meaning because of redemptive history, and redemptive history has meaning because of an interpreting word: "A revelatory word separated from the redeeming event is an abstraction; a saving event separated from the interpreting word is opaque."[37]

Jesus Christ is the definitive Word and Act of God. Scripture too is God's word-act. Yet, as we have seen, Ramm rejects the idea that biblical revelation is solely propositional, solely a matter of conveying information. Such a word-monism is reductionistic and fails to appreciate the dynamics of other literary genres in Scripture. If evangelical theology is at heart a form of interpretation, then it is incumbent upon the theologian to treat the various biblical texts according to their natures. Evangelicals must attend to all that God is doing in Scripture, from informing to promising to commanding, and so forth.

To find out what is in Scripture, Ramm advises the use of philology—all those skills necessary to interpret an ancient document. The etymology of *philology* ("love of words") is instructive, for the best interpreter of Scripture must have love (and faith, and hope) not only for the letter but for the gospel message that it communicates. Accordingly, evangelical biblical interpretation must be guided by a variation of the two principles examined above. Philologists must be Protestant, in the sense of ascribing priority to the meaning of the word-acts in Scripture rather than to one's own interpretations. Second, one's philological study of the Bible must acknowledge the centrality of Christology, that is, the overarching redemptive-historical plot and the climax of this plot in the life and work of Jesus Christ.

What every evangelical should know: Ramm the prophet

There are undoubtedly evangelicals to the left and to the right of what I have called Ramm's mature position. His challenge, both to conservatives and to progressives, is to give a comprehensive account for the authority structures that are often assumed but not always spelled out in their theologies. *The Evangelical Heritage* contributes to the current debate by stepping back from immediate disputes in order to position the evangelical movement against a wide historical backdrop. As such, the book contains a number of salient reminders of things that every evangelical should know. Moreover, the last two chapters include insights and exhortations that, even though originally addressed to evangelicals in the 1970s, continue to hit home with uncanny accuracy. We may therefore read *The Evangelical Heritage* as Ramm's prophetic word to today's evangelical theological community.

A prophet reminds the people of their covenant, or in this case their creedal and confessional, history. This is the burden of chapters 1 and 2, where Ramm traces the genesis of evangelical theology in ancient orthodoxy, as well as the exodus of evangelical theology, in the person of the Reformers, from the Roman Catholic Church.

Chapter 3 continues the story with an account of the "divided kingdom." Once settled in the promised land of Protestantism, evangelicals went their separate ways, with the more numerous part (the Arminians) eventually settling in the north, and the smaller tribes (the Calvinists) settling in Judah (or vice versa, depending on your theological allegiances!). Chapter 4 continues the narrative of the evangelical remnant in the guise of the Protestant scholastics.

Chapters 5–7 deal with the giants in the land—the Enlightenment, liberal, and neo-orthodox theologians—and with the ever-present danger of intermarriage of the two peoples. History shades into prophecy—forthtelling—in these chapters, as Ramm continues to remind the people of their evangelical obligations.

Ramm's narrative reaches a climax in Chapters 8 and 9, which we may liken to wisdom literature and apocalyptic respectively. Chapter 8 deserves to be read with great care, for it contains the distillation of a lifetime of experience and reflection on evangelical theology. More than that, it displays the truths at the heart of the evangelical heritage itself. It is in these pages that we find Ramm striving to articulate the essence of evangelical theology, mere evangelicalism. Ramm's efforts, though now some thirty years old, compare very favorably with more recent attempts to define evangelicalism. Newer is not always better.

Chapter 9 switches to another kind of prophetic genre, foretelling, as Ramm addresses the future of evangelical theology. What we find, however, is not a list of predictions so much as *prescriptions*. Ramm's five-point primer in evangelical theological method is worth presenting here in the introduction.

(1) Evangelicals must be students of Holy Scripture. Evangelical theology must proceed from the evangel—the God-given word about the God-given Christ—if it is truly to be built on divine revelation rather than on human speculation. Ramm is honest enough to admit that being "truly biblical" is one of the most difficult achievements, yet nothing less will do for evangelical theology. "The flow of thought must always be from the Scripture to the present situation."[38]

(2) Evangelicals must know the inner structure of evangelical theology. We have already dealt with Ramm's concern for questions of structural integrity, especially as these concern religious authority. It only remains to say that, for Ramm, the best way to understand the structure of evangelical theology is to know its heritage.

(3) Evangelicals must know their culture. Theology both shapes and is shaped by its age. This is another reason for becoming acquainted with the evangelical heritage. Ramm's main point, however, is that evangelicals must learn how to "exegete" their culture. Theologians who seek to minister the Word to the world must understand the art, literature, science, and philosophy of their day, not to mention its theology. This engagement with the wider world is part of what it means to be evangelical. The evangelical is to be salt and light in the world, not to build a ghetto. Evangelical theology has a built-in missional dimension.

(4) Evangelicals must be diligent students of language and communications. This point follows from the preceding one. Here Ramm truly was prescient; for our postmodern culture represents, among other things, a revolution in the philosophy of language. Moreover, new advances in technology and communications pose new questions to those who minister the Word in and through words. To be sure, evangelical theology has its own reasons for attending to language: the Bible is a linguistic phenomenon produced for commu-

nication.[39] Yet Ramm was surely right in emphasizing the central-ity of language and literature for doing evangelical theology in today's world.

(5) Evangelicals must rethink the manner in which God is related to the world. Here again, Ramm accurately foretells what has indeed become a burning issue within evangelical theology itself: the "openness" of God. Ramm, of course, is unable to help us with the specifics of this rethinking, though he is clear that what we must not do is capitulate to the modern (or postmodern) mentality. Instead, we should work for "a restatement or reformulation or reconceptualization of the biblical message about God, the world, and transcendence, which does not surrender the uniqueness of the scriptural revelation and at the same time remains in real commu-nication with [our] own generation."[40] Ramm speculates that, when all is said and done, we may conclude that what Luther or Calvin had to say on this matter continues to be the most satisfactory. For at its best, the evangelical heritage is not a shrine to the past, but a beacon in the present.

Conclusion

Ramm's corpus is now part of the evangelical heritage itself. That does not, of course, make it infallible. Ramm knew only too well that evangelical theology must not presume that the final or near-final statement of Christian theology has been achieved, nor does it need such an assumption. Just as the Christian life requires not simply one righteous act but a lifetime of obedience, so too Chris-tian theology demands not just one correct thought but a continual rethinking. Nevertheless, if we are not to start from scratch, guide-books will be needed.

The Evangelical Heritage never became the textbook that others of Ramm's books did. Yet it deserves to be on every evangelical seminary student's required reading list, not because it takes us all the way, but because it keeps us going in the right direction. Ramm is not the one to provide the definitive solution to the problems of postmodernity; evangelicalism must wait for another. Yet like the namesake of his denomination, Ramm's voice continues to cry out for evangelical theology to make its path straight, to prepare the way of the Lord.

NOTES

1. Bernard Ramm, *After Fundamentalism: The Future of Evangelical Theology* (San Francisco: Harper & Row, 1983), 1.

2. Mark Noll, *The Scandal of the Evangelical Mind* (Grand Rapids, Mich.: Eerdmans, 1995).

3. David Wells, *No Place for Truth or Whatever Happened to Evangelical Theology?* (Grand Rapids, Mich.: Eerdmans, 1993).

4. See, for example, Dennis Okholm and Timothy Phillips, eds., *The Nature of Confession: Evangelicals and Postliberals in Conversation* (Downers Grove, Ill.: InterVarsity Press, 1996).

5. See, for example, D. M. Lloyd-Jones, *What is an Evangelical?* (Edinburgh: Banner of Truth Trust, 1992), a series of lectures originally delivered in 1971.

6. See Christopher A. Hall, *Reading Scripture with the Church Fathers* (Downers Grove, Ill.: InterVarsity Press, 1998).

7. Thomas C. Oden, gen. ed., *Ancient Christian Commentary on Scripture* (Downers Grove, Ill.: InterVarsity, 1998–).

8. Bernard Ramm, *The Christian View of Science and Scripture* (Grand Rapids, Mich.: Eerdmans, 1955), 48. It is true that Ramm tends to privilege the Reformers over the church fathers, but it should not be forgotten that the Reformers themselves had a healthy respect for patristic thought, and especially for Augustine. See also Robert E. Webber's attempt to link the evangelical heritage, rooted in the ancient church, to the postmodern situation, *Ancient-Future Faith: Rethinking Evangelicalism for a Postmodern World* (Grand Rapids, Mich.: Baker, 1999).

9. The seminal texts are John Milbank, *Theology and Social Theory: Beyond Secular Reason* (Oxford: Blackwell, 1990) and John Milbank, Catherine Pickstock, and Graham Ward, eds., *Radical Orthodoxy* (London: Routledge, 1999).

10. Ramm, *After Fundamentalism*, 176.

11. *Evangelical Heritage*, 132.

12. See William Stacy Johnson, *The Mystery of God: Karl Barth and the Postmodern Foundations of Theology* (Louisville, Ky.: Westminster/John Knox, 1997).

13. *Evangelical Heritage*, 154–55.

14. J. Gresham Machen, *Christianity and Liberalism* (New York: Macmillan, 1923).

15. It should be noted that the later Barth—the author of *Church Dogmatics*—broke with what is usually called "neo-orthodoxy." For a thorough study of this point, see Bruce L. McCormack, *Karl Barth's Critically Realistic Dialectical Theology: Its Genesis and Development, 1909–1936* (Oxford: Clarendon Press, 1995).

16. Clark H. Pinnock, *Tracking the Maze: Finding Our Way Through Modern Theology from an Evangelical Perspective* (San Francisco: Harper & Row, 1990).

17. Millard J. Erickson, *The Evangelical Left: Encountering Postconservative Evangelical Theology* (Grand Rapids, Mich.: Baker, 1997), esp. pp. 33–38.

18. Roger E. Olson, "Postconservative Evangelicals Greet the Postmodern

Age," *Christian Century* 112.15 (May 3, 1995), 480. The characteristics include: eagerness to dialogue with nonevangelical theologians; recognition of the influence of social location on one's theological work; a broadening of the sources used in theology; a discontent with the traditional evangelical tie to common-sense realism; an emphasis on biblical narrative rather than on propositions; an "open view" of God; a hope for a near-universal salvation; a more synergistic understanding of salvation.

19. I admit that the thinking in this paragraph represents an educated guess. Considerably more research would have to be done to confirm my hypothesis. I shall return to the question of Barth's influence on Ramm below.

20. I have tried to correct an unnecessary confusion that often prevents evangelicals from hearing what Barth is saying in my "God's Mighty Speech Acts: The Doctrine of Scripture Today," in Philip E. Satterthwaite and D. F. Wright, eds., *A Pathway into the Holy Scripture* (Grand Rapids, Mich.: Eerdmans, 1994), 143–81.

21. Bernard Ramm, "Helps from Karl Barth," in Donald K. McKim, ed., *How Karl Barth Changed My Mind* (Grand Rapids, Mich.: Eerdmans, 1986), 121–25.

22. Bernard Ramm apparently repents of his earlier apologetic studies, a species of evidentialism, by speaking of "the futility and intellectual bankruptcy of my former strategy" ("Helps from Karl Barth," 121). While it is not clear that Ramm ever espoused a postfoundationalist epistemology, it is clear that he felt the force of the critique of epistemological objectivism that later proved to be an easy target for a number of postmodern thinkers.

23. Ramm, "Helps from Karl Barth," 125.

24. Bernard Ramm, *The Witness of the Spirit* (Grand Rapids, Mich.: Eerdmans, 1959), 124.

25. Bernard Ramm, *The Pattern of Religious Authority* (Grand Rapids, Mich.: Eerdmans, 1957), 29.

26. Ibid., 28.

27. Erickson, *The Evangelical Left*, 78.

28. I have tried to explicate what Barth may have meant in terms of speech act theory. In terms of the objective content of Scripture (the locutions and illocutions), the Bible is God's Word. In terms of the subjective effect (the perlocutions), the Bible becomes God's Word only when the Spirit convicts the reader. Apart from these conceptual distinctions, however, Barth and evangelicals could only talk past one another. See my "God's Mighty Speech Acts" (n. 20 above.)

29. Postmodern exegetes and theologians have stressed the importance of the imagination, too. See, for instance, Walter Brueggemann, *Texts under Negotiation: The Bible and Postmodern Imagination* (Philadelphia: Fortress, 1993).

30. Ramm, *Evangelical Heritage*, 130.

31. Ibid.

32. Ibid., 131.

33. Bernard Ramm, *Special Revelation and the Word of God* (Grand Rapids, Mich.: Eerdmans, 1961), 117.

34. Ramm, *Evangelical Heritage*, 119. There is doubtless ample scope for a doctoral dissertation on the topic of Ramm's complicated, even dialectical, relationship to the theology of Karl Barth.

35. Ramm, *Pattern of Religious Authority*, 37.
36. Ramm, *Evangelical Heritage,* 13.
37. Ramm, *Special Revelation and the Word of God*, 82.
38. Ramm, *Evangelical Heritage,* 152.
39. Ramm's remark "that the next impetus to rethink our evangelical doctrines of inspiration and revelation is going to come from the modern communications theory" (ibid., 163) is particularly interesting in light of postmodern developments. I have tried, in my own work, to rethink the doctrine of Scripture and biblical interpretation in terms of contemporary linguistics, literary theory, and communication studies in my *Is There a Meaning in this Text? The Bible, the Reader, and the Morality of Literary Knowledge* (Grand Rapids, Mich.: Zondervan, 1998).
40. Ramm, *Evangelical Heritage*, 169.

Chapter One

EVANGELICAL THEOLOGY BELONGS TO THE CHRISTIAN WEST

Section 1: The purpose of a study of theological geography

How many evangelicals are there in America? Did religious liberalism, neoorthodoxy, Bultmannism, and other recent theological movements reduce the evangelical population to a remnant? The answers to these questions and their implications are at the heart of what I wish to say in this book. *United States News and World Report* [1] estimates that there are forty to forty-five million evangelicals in America. This report does not make all evangelicals happy, for a number of cultic groups, which evangelicals do not believe belong to the evangelical camp, were included in this figure. Discounting these cultic groups lowers the total figure by some millions but certainly not lower than around thirty-five million.

On the other hand, the report said that one third of these evangelicals belong to main-line churches, but that runs counter to another study. Rodney Stark and Charles Glock studied theological commitments of the major denominations in America.[2] In a series of charts that generally outlined the range of theological beliefs from extreme liberalism to robust orthodoxy, Stark and Glock showed that laymen in our larger denominations registered rather consistently at 85 percent or above in favor of orthodox beliefs. Although these charts are not easily interpreted, they nevertheless suggest that the statement by *United States News and World Report* that one-third of the evangelicals are in the main-line denominations is realistically far too small.

To state precisely the exact head count of evangelicals in America is unnecessary. The figures do, however, show that rather than being a small handful of crank holdouts from the nineteenth century evangelicals number in the tens of millions. This very fact must be reckoned with by American churchmen.[3]

When Helmut Thielicke of the theological faculty of the University of Hamburg visited America, he summed up his impressions in a book titled *Between Heaven and Earth*. As he preached, taught, lectured, and traveled the length and width of the land, he became acutely aware of the great number of fundamentalists and evangelicals. His evaluation of the situation in the American churches led him to become fearful that the American denominations would steadily crowd out the fundamentalists and evangelicals. He notes with sadness "how often they [evangelicals] are criticized from the high horse of Enlightenment and then, naturally, are unfairly dealt with." [4] He continues:

> If American Christianity loses these people, who are often the most vital members of its body [as the Stark and Glock survey revealed]— if it should, say, drive them into sectarianism and thus allow them to die away—this could be fatal to its cause. Therefore, where it was possible, I tried to call attention to these questions and blow the horn as loud as I could.[5]

Thielicke's words must be taken with maximum seriousness. He was one of the few men who resisted Hitler and consented to the plot for Hitler's assassination. Thielicke was saved because his name came at the fold of the paper of the list of betrayers and had become illegible through the course of many foldings.

When World War II was over and Germany lay prostrate in every way, but worst of all, in spirit, the man who stood up to rally the spirits of the German people was Thielicke. At the University of Tübingen, with its largest auditorium so packed with students he could hardly reach the lectern and with loud speakers carrying his voice to two other halls, he attempted to give these students new hope so that they would not be swallowed up in the whirlpool of nihilism.[6]

Thielicke continues to reach the common man in Germany. Once a month he preaches in Hamburg to a church full of the ordinary people of the city. So unusual and evangelical are these sermons that already a small library of them have been translated and published in English.

He is no less distinguished for his academic achievements. His *Theological Ethics,* published in many volumes and now being translated into English, is one of the most grandiose works in the history of Christian ethics.

If this man says that one of the biggest blunders the American church can make is to miscalculate the strength and importance of the fundamentalists and evangelicals, then it appears, in my judgment, that American churchmen who ignore Thielicke's advice are sinfully careless of their stewardship in the church of Jesus Christ.

Where Thielicke has used the expression *fundamentalist,* I have used the terms *fundamentalist* and *evangelical.* Unfortunately the word *fundamentalist* suggests to many people a rancorous theological weed which they wish would die off. Because the word has picked up such odious connotations, other words have been substituted such as conservative, historic, neoevangelical, or evangelical. Therefore, to keep the dialogue going, I have in general used the word *evangelical* to include both fundamentalists and evangelicals.

It is impossible to give one, neat, precise definition of an evangelical. At the headwaters of all efforts to define the true version of Christianity is that of Vincent of Lerins (died about A.D. 450). His *Vincentian Canon* defined orthodoxy as "what has been believed everywhere [ecumenicity], always [antiquity], and by all [consent]." There are too many variations in the early church for this canon to be a reliable definition of orthodoxy. In the most general sense, evangelical Christianity refers to that version of Christianity which places the priority of the Word and Act of God over the faith, response, or experiences of men. Concretely this means the supremacy and authority of the Word of God (as a synonym for all the revelations of God, written and unwritten) over all human philosophies or religions. Truth in the garments of theology is prior to, and more fundamental than, faith or experience.

This also means that paralleling the divine Word is the divine Act —Creation, the call of Abraham, the Exodus, the Incarnation, the cross, the Resurrection, and the descent of the Spirit. The Word of God and the Act of God compenetrate so that it is artificial to separate them in any manner.

In the language of textbook theology this difference has been stated by using two Latin expressions. Faith as that objective thing which exists before men, and which God has done for men, has been indicated by the expression *fides quae creditur.* Faith as man's personal response to God's revelation and salvation is expressed as *fides qua creditur*. Both Roman Catholic theology and historic Protestant orthodoxy have insisted on the priority of faith as object over against faith as attitude. The fateful reversal of these two expressions of the word *faith* was made by Schleiermacher who is generally considered the theological father of liberalism.

The use of the term *evangelical* will then be flexible. It will include the obscurantistic fundamentalist and the learned Lutheran or Reformed confessional theologian. It includes the Pentecostals who, in spite of their emphasis on experience to the neglect of theology and biblical interpretation, nevertheless hold to the historic doctrines of the church. It also includes a person who might bear such a vague title as an evangelical neoorthodox.

To come at the matter of definition from another direction, it may be said that the essence of liberalism or modernism and other non-evangelical theologies is that religion is primarily the religious experiences of man or the religious potential of man or the religious a priori in man. Faith as an inward stance or attitude toward religion is to the liberal more fundamental than faith as the dogmatic expression of Christianity. Hence, in religious liberalism the Scripture is normative in the stratum that speaks of a religious experience, and Christ is normative as the God-filled man, or the adopted Son of God, or the *Urbild* (archetype) of the truly religious man. Or, as Fosdick expressed it so many times, Christianity is about the kind of piety and morality that Jesus practiced and not about the dogmatic contents of the New Testament.

As previously noted this reversal of the relationship of faith to truth, or faith to theology, stems from Schleiermacher and is to the evangelical a fatal reconstruction of the Christian faith.

Some evangelicals have a good grasp of the history of evangelical theology. Unfortunately, the majority is sadly deficient in historical knowledge. Their theology tends to be ahistorical. They lack a sense of the course of theological history which is their heritage. They believe what they are taught here-and-now and have no awareness of the there-and-before. To hold evangelical faith without a minimal knowledge of its history is theologically unhealthy if not precarious. Without question, a number of fundamentalists and evangelicals have deserted the camp because, lacking any real historical knowledge of their heritage, they did not see their heritage in its proper light nor did they have an appropriate vantage point from which to assess the alternative view to which they capitulated.

An evangelical who holds an ahistorical faith has no real sense of the theological and spiritual continuity of his faith. The church is the body of Christ not only for the first centuries but for all centuries. The very concept of the church as the body of Christ implies historical continuity. The unity of the Spirit (Eph. 4:3) implies the continuity of the Spirit. Having a sense of one's historical roots gives one a sense of being a member of the body of Christ, the company of believers of all centuries, and of keeping both the unity and continuity of the Holy Spirit. This sense of continuity—of sharing in a heritage of theology and life, of faith and action—is an integral part of deep Christian conviction. It is having a sense of the Tradition amidst traditions.

An evangelical with an ahistorical faith is a superficial Christian. Is this too strong a judgment?

How can an evangelical who has not refought the battle of Augustine and Pelagius have a real understanding of the Christian doctrine of sin? Or the same contest over the nature of sin between the Reformers and the Roman Catholic church? Or the famous exchange of books on the subject between Erasmus and Luther?

How can an evangelical who has not followed the christological controversies of the early church have a mature view of the person of Christ? What were the differences between Arius and Athanasius? What do the strange Greek words *homoousia, anhypostasis,* and *enhypostasis* mean? And why do the Calvinists and Lutherans oppose each other over the *extra-Calvinisticum?* Why did a strong kenotic controversy develop in the nineteenth century (Thomasius, Gess, Gore), and what bearing did it have on biblical criticism? The Council of Nicaea affirmed the deity of Christ as God the Son and the Council of Chalcedon drew the lines bracketing the doctrine of the incarnation. Can the decisions of these councils be defended today?

The Christian sacraments are a part of Christian worship. But what is a sacrament? Can an evangelical come to a really responsible decision without knowing the treatment of the seven sacraments by Thomas Aquinas in his *Summa Theologica?* The unity of the Reformation was permanently split at the Colloquy of Marburg in 1529 when Luther and Zwingli differed fundamentally over the meaning of the Lord's Supper. Did Calvin successfully breach the division by the introduction of the presence of the Holy Spirit in the sacraments? Does the evangelical know the greatest sacramental theologian of the Reformation—Peter Martyr Vermigli?

What does it mean to be a Protestant? Can an evangelical really
be theologically on the inside of Protestantism without having pored
over the doctrinal segments of the *Decrees of the Council of Trent*
and seeing what the Roman Catholic position was in contrast to that
of the Protestant Reformers? And is not a reading of Melanchthon's
Apology for the famous Augsburg Confession of 1530 necessary to
understand why Protestant Lutherans could accept some Roman
Catholic theology but at certain points had to part company in good
Protestant conscience?

What is said above is not to minimize the study of Scripture or the
study of biblical interpretation or the study of biblical theology. All
of these studies are central for Protestant faith, but unless these studies are seen historically and understood by historical crises in the
church they will be perceived too academically.

But how does one attack this disease of being ahistorical from
which evangelicals suffer? Through an approach which is basically
historical—for how else does one correct the ahistorical but with
history? *The Evangelical Heritage* will attempt to trace the history
of evangelicalism through the great theological crises of the church.
This is not an evangelical version of the "trail of blood" theory of the
"apostolic succession" of the Baptist church. It does not intend to see
historical theology through such prejudiced glasses. For this reason
it is a geography and not a history. A history of evangelical theology
would presume a silver thread of evangelical theology traceable in the
whole history of the theology of the church. A geography of evangelical theology points out the evangelical's stake at certain great
historical divisions in theology which eventually does lead to the
emergence of and articulation of an evangelical Protestant theology.

Section 2: The different mentalities of the East and West

The great empires of man began in Asia and Egypt. From archeological records and from biblical history, we learn that empire succeeded empire. However, the fateful day came when the Greeks of
the West faced off with the Persians of the East. The conquests of the
Eastern lands by Alexander the Great brought the center of civilization from Asia to Europe. Not many years later a stronger empire
even farther west, the Roman Empire, spread throughout the East
and the West.

A map of the ancient Roman Empire during the height of its geographical spread looks as if all that ancient world was bound together

in one unified confederation. But this is a mirage, for the map fails to convey the enormous diversity that persisted in the Roman Empire. Underneath the apparent unity was a great cultural division of the East and the West. Eventually under Theodosius I the Roman Empire was divided into two parts (A.D. 395). The capital of the East was Constantinople; Rome continued as the capital of the West. The line of demarcation was not the Bosporus which divides Europe and Asia but the waters between Italy and Greece.

The Christian church, originating in Palestine, eventually followed the contours of the Roman Empire and spread south and west into Egypt and North Africa and north and west into Europe.[7] However, just as an East-West division lay underneath the apparent unity of the Roman Empire, the same division lay underneath the apparent unity of the patristic church. Eventually the cultural dissimilarity which divided the Roman Empire would divide the Christian church also. Of course, on the surface the division is reported as being theological, and that theological elements were part of the divergence need not be denied.

A long and complicated story must be short-cut. Eventually the East and West split into the Roman Catholic Church of the West and the Holy Orthodox Apostolic Eastern (or Oriental) Church. There are other orthodox churches in the East, but our concern is with this central division.

Cultural and theological differences became most apparent and were intensified by the brilliant theologian of the Eastern church, Photius (A.D. 810–95?). He was the author of the important work, *The Mystagogy of the Holy Spirit*. The formal division of the Roman and the Eastern church came in A.D. 1054.

The evangelical is in the tradition of the Roman West in this split. The Reformers were born, raised, and educated in the world dominated by the Roman Catholic church. Although they broke away, nevertheless their cultural, educational, and theological mother was the Roman Catholic West. It is therefore of central evangelical concern to understand the differences between the East and the West and to see our heritage as it emerges from the West.

Section 3: The doctrinal differences between the East and West

The East and the West have in common a number of doctrines and practices, including the seven sacraments, the authority of councils and Fathers, and the genuine participation of the church in the mediation of salvation. Our concern is with the differences. The highest count of the differences I have encountered is sixty. Most of these were secondary matters of liturgy and church order. Our concern is with major differences.

The Eastern church is more mystical; the Western church, more rational. The word *more* is used purposefully. There is a rational element in the Eastern church and a mystical tradition in the Western church. The difference lies in where the stress comes, and coming at different points in each church, it creates two different mentalities.

The Eastern church thinks doctrines are to be adored as mysteries and not analyzed or rationalized. The result has been that the Eastern church has never developed the enormous body of theological literature characteristic of the Western church. In fact, its theology had almost stagnated after John of Damascus (A.D. 675–749) whose writings form the fundamental basis of the theology of the Eastern church.

The Western church was far more influenced by the rational and analytical aspects of Greek philosophy, and those great theologians like Tertullian and Augustine were rhetoricians or lawyers. It could be said that this rational impulse in the Western church reached its acme in the huge *Summa Theologica* of Thomas Aquinas.

On the other hand, the mystical emphasis in the East had other outcroppings. The Eastern church is liturgical in the fullest sense of the word. In the liturgy, heaven comes down to earth. There is no real center of the liturgy as in the act of transubstantiation of bread and wine into the body and blood of Christ as in the Western church, but heaven is there equally throughout the entire liturgy. This intense emphasis on the liturgical with its roots in the mysterious and the mystical is not conducive to theological curiosity. Furthermore, the Eastern church is gathered up into *sobornost* in worship. This word is considered untranslatable, but it contains the ideas of communion, fellowship, rapport, and oneness of spirit. By virtue of *sobornost,* the priest and people in the Eastern church feel far more as one in Christ than in the Western church where the division of clergy and laity is pronounced.

The Western church is governed by the pope; the Eastern, by patriarchs. The Roman Catholic church believes that in Matthew 16 Jesus made Peter the bishop of bishops, the universal bishop of the church. Peter's papal authority goes with him, and where he resides is the see (from Latin, *sedes,* a throne) of the papacy. When Peter went to Rome, he thereby established the papal see at Rome. For this reason the Western church is called the Roman Catholic church. When the pope speaks from his see, that is, *ex cathedra*—from his official chair as the universal teacher of the church—he speaks infallibly to all the church. Although this was not defined until Vatican I in 1870, it is presumed that it was a power of the papacy beginning with Peter.

The Eastern church rejects the papacy. Five cities were considered special cities by the early church because it was believed that an apostle was the bishop of the church in that city. Those cities were Jerusalem, Rome, Alexandria, Antioch, and Constantinople. The bishops who succeeded the apostles in these five special cities were called patriarchs. The particular title *patriarch,* however, is not found earlier than the sixth century. The patriarch was somewhat of a pope within his region except that his authority was that of governing and not of giving infallible teaching about points of doctrine. The patriarchs are all considered equal although the Eastern church will grant that the patriarch of Rome is first among equals.

Many older Protestants did not believe that Peter ever came to Rome. In recent times Oscar Cullmann has amassed sufficient evidence to convince most Protestants that Peter, as a matter of fact, did come to Rome.[8] The suggestion by Roman Catholics that recent excavations have unearthed the very bones of Peter is not considered established on sound archeological principles.[9]

The Western church teaches salvation by infusion; the Eastern church, by deification. Both churches are sacramental. Both believe that sacraments are the causes and channels of God's grace. Each sacrament has its substance, its specific words, and its liturgy. Both churches have seven sacraments. But here the similarity stops.

The Roman Catholic church understands salvation to be an infusion of sanctifying or saving grace. It sounds odd to Protestants unfamiliar with Roman Catholic theology, but infused or sanctifying grace is justification, regeneration, and sanctification rolled into one. The justification of the sinner is a bestowal of a righteous quality to the soul itself.

The Eastern church believes in salvation by deification. This is not an easy concept to grasp. Man was made in the image of God. If sin is the loss of the image, then salvation is the restoration of the image. Deification is the act of grace and of salvation which restores the image of God. It can be put another way. Just as God became man for our salvation, man becomes deified when he is saved. As synonyms for deification Benz [10] uses such terms as fulfillment, renewal, transfiguration, perfection, and apotheosis. The idea of partaking of the divine nature (2 Pet. 1:4) is taken quite literally. The new birth is also interpreted as a deification of man.

So strong has been this emphasis on liturgy, mystery, and deification that the concept of salvation by justification doesn't occur in the early theological history of the Eastern church. It starts to crop up only after the Roman Catholic-Protestant debate over the nature of justification.

The Western church accepts the filioque; *the Eastern church rejects it.* The first great theological struggle of the Christian church was whether Jesus Christ was God in the same sense that God the Father is God or whether Jesus was God in some secondary sense. The defender of the belief that Jesus is God in an undiminished sense as the Father is God was Athanasius. His opponent was Arius who said that Jesus was God in a secondary or derived sense. He was the first and highest creation of God through whom God created all things and hence could be called a second god. The issue was settled at the Council of Nicaea (325) although the usual form of the Nicene Creed used in churches is that of Nicaea-Constantinople (381).

In the following centuries, with the victory of Athanasius over Arius, there was still a certain amount of Arian static. There was apparently much static in Spain, for in speaking of the procession of the Holy Spirit from the Father (stated in the Nicaea-Constantinople Creed), the Spaniards added the word *filioque*. The first official appearance of *filioque* was in the findings of the Third Council of Toledo (589).

The Latin word for son is *filius,* and one of the words for and is *que. Filioque* translated is "and the son." This means that the Holy Spirit proceeds not only from the Father as the Nicene Creed stated but also proceeds from the Son. The Western church accepted the word *filioque* into the Nicene Creed [11] whereas the Eastern church not only did not accept it but strenuously objected to its addition.

The Eastern church objected on two grounds: (1) Once a council has set the wording of a creed, it is wrong to alter it in any way. (2) Serious theological errors follow from adding *filioque*. It leads to a wrong notion of the Trinity, for with *filioque* the Father is not the fountainhead of the Trinity but the Father and Son are. To append the Spirit to the Father and the Son in this manner is to alter radically one's understanding of the Spirit and his work in the world.

There is an enormous literature on *filioque*.[12] To some church historians it is a false issue because they consider the real issue between the churches to have been political and not theological. Although the Eastern church used *filioque* as its basis for dividing from the Western church, it was a surface excuse. But to others its addition was a necessary step in more fully understanding the Trinity just as the Eastern theologians believe it was a betrayal of the Trinity.

Photius (810–95) was one of the greatest theologians of the Eastern church, and he made a powerful attack on the addition of *filioque* and stoutly defended the Eastern position. On the Protestant side the classic defense for *filioque* was made by E. B. Pusey in his work, *On the Clause "And the Son"* (1876). In modern times it has been defended by Barth in much detail.[13] Barth retains the *filioque* on the basis that it protects the christological character of the New Testament doctrine of the Spirit. There can be no Pneumatology (doctrine of the Spirit) without a foregoing Christology.

There isn't any official Protestant or evangelical view on *filioque* except that the form of the Nicaea-Constantinople Creed as adopted by the Roman Catholic church was taken over by Protestant churches at the Reformation and from that lineage to contemporary evangelicals.

In summary, then, Protestant churches are heirs, theologically speaking, of the Western church and not the Eastern church. Protestant theology reflects accordingly much more the theological mentality of the Western church than the Eastern church, and in certain important doctrinal matters stands with the West against the East. The contemporary evangelical who is heir to the Protestant heritage stands then in the same stance in the East-West division as did the Reformers and their children in the second and third Protestant generations from the Reformation.

NOTES

1. "New Life for Old Time Religion," *United States News and World Report,* 19 October 1970, pp. 84–87.
2. Rodney Stark and Charles Glock, *American Piety: The Nature of Religious Commitment* (Berkeley, Cal.: University of California Press, 1968).
3. Stark and Glock state that one of the most obvious results of their research was that a corrosion of real commitment accompanied the rise

of modernized and liberalized theology (see p. 213 in *American Piety*).
It is also evident from their study that the highest percentage of liberalism
occurs in the seminaries; the next highest percentage occurs among pastors. Stark and Glock indicate that American orthodoxy is declining, but
United States News and World Report said that evangelical groups were
increasing in number by about 3 percent a year whereas main-line
denominational membership is declining.

    4. Quoted in Stark and Glock, *American Piety*, p. xv.

    5. Ibid., p. xvi.

    6. These lectures were published and translated into English, appearing as *Nihilism: Its Origin and Nature—with a Christian Answer* (New
York: Schocken Books, 1969).

    7. For a general discussion of these issues see Hans-Georg Beck,
"Byzantine Empire," *Sacramentum Mundi: An Encyclopedia of Theology*, ed. K. Rahner (New York: Herder & Herder, 1968) 1:242–46.

    8. Oscar Cullman, *Peter: Disciple, Apostle, Martyr*, trans. V. F. Wilson, 2d rev. ed. (Philadelphia: Westminster, 1962).

    9. Ibid., pp. 131 ff.

    10. E. Benz, *The Eastern Orthodox Church*, trans. R. & C. Winston
(Chicago: Aldin, 1963), p. 51. See also Timothy Ware, *The Orthodox
Church* (Magnolia, Mass.: Peter Smith, 1963), p. 51.

    11. See "Council of Florence, 1439–45," D, 691. "D" stands for the
number paragraph in H. Denzinger's collection of the official pronouncements of the papacy and the Roman Catholic church *(Enchiridion Symbolorum Definitionum et Declarationum de Rebus Fidei et Morum)*.

    12. See Karl Barth's materials in *The Doctrine of the Word of God,
Church Dogmatics*, I/1 (Edinburgh: T. & T. Clark, 1936), pp. 541 ff.
The official English edition of *Church Dogmatics* is cited hereafter as
C.D. with appropriate volume numbers.

    13. Ibid., pp. 546 ff.

Chapter Two

EVANGELICAL THEOLOGY
BELONGS TO
REFORMATION THEOLOGY

Section 4: The development of the Roman Catholic church

As the Eastern and Western churches gradually pulled apart, the Western church began to develop a life, liturgy, and theological pattern of its own. The Western church became known as the Roman Catholic church because Peter, the first pope, died in Rome, establishing Rome as the official papal see. There is a legend which says that when Peter saw the persecution of Christians in Rome he fled the city. In flight he met Christ going in the opposite direction. Peter said to Christ, *Domine quo vadis?* "Lord, where are you going?" Christ answered, "I am to be crucified again." Peter understood this to mean that his Lord was going to Rome to be crucified again for him. Smitten in heart, he returned to Rome and was crucified.[1] He was then succeeded by Linus.[2]

It was the conviction of the Reformers that the Roman Catholic church of the sixteenth century was not the same as the early, undivided patristic church but a development of the Middle Ages. Among the more important developments in the Roman Catholic church during the Middle Ages were:

The doctrine of the pope as the successor of Peter and universal head of the church was fully established. Boniface VIII in his bull, *Unam Sanctam* (18 November 1302), said that unless a person were in communion with the pope he could not be saved.

The sacramental system was expanded to seven sacraments and given a sustained theological defense in Thomas Aquinas's Summa Theologica.

23

Mary the Mother of God as a title indicating the reality of the incarnation was systematically reinterpreted to mean that Mary, as the new Eve, participates in the plan of redemption. That is to say, a Marian theology developed.

The universities were founded, and out of them came a typical kind of scholarship that characterized the medieval theologians. It is known as scholasticism, and at the time of the Reformation it was in a degenerate form and receiving strong competition from the humanistic scholarship stemming from the Renaissance.

The allegorical method of interpreting the Scriptures, so popular with many of the Fathers and somewhat codified by Augustine, led to the four-fold theory of biblical interpretation. Every passage of Scripture may have four interpretations: literal or historical; moral or spiritual; allegorical or prophetic or typological; and eschatological or heavenly.

There was a sustained discussion over the relationship of faith and reason or philosophy and revelation or nature and grace. Part of the result of this was the heavy interlarding of philosophical elements in scholastic theology. The general or prevailing assumption was that "grace does not contradict but perfects and completes nature [or creation]." The Reformers seriously challenged this position.

A specific Roman Catholic piety developed in the Middle Ages. The Catholic believer saw himself as a poor sinner, a pilgrim passing through dangerous terrain. Suffering, poverty, and self-denial were heavenly scourges to increase his spirituality. Great emphasis was laid on the physical sufferings of Christ with the pictures of the "bleeding heart" and the "pieta"—the dead Christ in the arms of Mary. Indulgences came into existence and developed into both a boon to the guilt-burdened Catholic and to the financial benefit of the church. The sacrament of penance became operationally the most important sacrament, for in penance the Catholic believer and the priest met on personal terms wherein the spiritual life of the individual was governed, controlled, and profoundly influenced. It was this combination of the sacrament of penance and the sale of indulgences that compelled Luther to break with the Roman Catholic church.

Section 5: The Reformers set the Word of God above the church

From this point on I shall record the major differences between the Reformers and the Roman Catholic church. In each of these points the evangelical of today is with the Reformers as against Roman Catholic theology. The first difference arose over the question of how the Word of God and the church are to be related.

According to Roman Catholic theology Jesus Christ brought the original revelation upon which the church and the New Testament are founded. This is called the Tradition, and at first it existed only in oral form in the speeches or teachings of Christ. It was preserved in the memories of the apostles after the ascension, and they in turn taught the church the Tradition. Because of the various needs of the different churches, the apostles began writing. The original Tradition then split into two streams: written Tradition or Holy Scripture, specifically the New Testament; oral Tradition in the form of the witness of the apostles delivered to the churches and customarily designated by the word *tradition*. The reader should note carefully that Tradition with a capital *T* indicates the total revelation that came through Christ; tradition with the lower case *t* indicates the primeval Tradition in its oral form as deposited within the Roman Catholic church.

The Roman Catholic church preserves the Tradition in both its written and unwritten forms. By grace given to it of God (especially in that it is indwelt by both Christ and the Spirit), it can recognize the Word of God. It, therefore, has the grace to define what books are inspired and may then form the official canon of the Old and New Testaments. In a real sense the church is prior to the New Testament as it bears first the original Tradition, and it can be said then that the church gives the New Testament to the church. (It must be stated at this point that I am comparing Protestantism with the status of Roman Catholic theology at the time of the Reformation. Recent changes in the Roman Catholic church have made some of these differences obsolete and others have been seriously modified.)

No one debates the idea that between the ascension of Christ and the first Christian writings the churches lived by oral tradition. Nor does anybody doubt that the churches meeting in council designated the canon of the New Testament (Rome, under Pope Damasus, A.D. 382, the Gelasian Decree).

The question the Reformers asked was: What formed the church from its inception? Their answer was that the church cannot form itself. In general terms the Word of God, and in specific terms the gospel, forms the church. The written canon is but the congealing of the prior existing Word of God. Although coming after in point of time of the beginning of the church at Pentecost, the canon is logically and in point of authority prior to the church or above the church. The church does not give itself the Word of God; it can only recognize within itself what is the Word of God. The Catholic position is an odd one in that it presumes that the church can exist prior to the Word of God when the church by its very definition can exist only by virtue of the prior Word of God. Thus, the emergence of the church prior to the formation of the New Testament canon is of no theological significance to the Reformers, for to grant it significance would require turning everything on its head.

Furthermore, it is the Word of God which nourishes, feeds, and sustains the church. The church may well be the custodian of Scripture, but it is Scripture that rules the custodian and not the custodian, Scripture. The church is not to be the lord and master of the Scripture, but the Scripture is to be the critic of the church: "For the word of God is living and active, sharper than any two-edged sword, piercing to the division of soul and spirit, of joints and marrow, and discerning the thoughts and intentions of the heart" (Heb. 4:12).

Cardinal Sadolet wrote a letter to the city of Geneva in an attempt to win it away from the Reformers and back to the Roman Catholic church. In his famous *Reply to Sadolet,* Calvin so argued, with that genius that was peculiar to him, that the church was under the Word, and not the Word under the church, that Sadolet's appeal achieved nothing in the city of Geneva.

Section 6: The Reformers claimed that the Scriptures contained their own power of self-authentication

To understand this point the reader must not think of the present stance within the Roman Catholic church, especially after Vatican II, but he must project himself backward in time to the Reformation. It taught then that the only basis for the Roman Catholic to know that there was a Word of God, that Scripture was that Word of God, and therefore that he could be sure he had the Word was through the teaching magisterium of the Roman Catholic church. Tersely put, the Roman Catholic church identified the Holy Bible as the Word of God. Without that validation, no man could know with certainty that the Bible was the Word of God.

The position of the Reformers was that if the Word of God required an external certification it was not inherently the Word of God. As Amos put it, just as the roar of the lion self-validates the lion as a lion, so the Word of God validates itself as the Word of God (Amos 4:8). Among the Reformers, Calvin did the most creative thinking on this subject. He asks how the tongue knows that sugar is sugar. The answer is that the sweetness of sugar which is the essence of sugar is the validation of sugar. Salt validates itself by its saltiness. In like manner, the Word of God validates itself.

But what is the sweetness or saltiness of Scripture which when tasted validates Scripture as the Word of God? To Calvin this quality was majesty. The model behind this concept seems to be that of a king although Calvin does not state this concept in these words. The king by being a king can utter an imperial word, so God as the imperial King of the universe utters his imperial Word which reflects his imperial majesty, and the human spirit (as we shall note shortly, by the aid of the Divine Spirit) recognizes this majesty and so knows it is the Word of God. Luther taught that it was the power of the Word of God which was its authenticating characteristic. Either way, both Reformers taught the power of Scripture to validate itself as the Word of God apart from the verdict of the church—although the historical continuity of that verdict within the church was no small thing to Calvin.

The Reformers argued that the Word of God being inherently the Word of God makes its own way as the Word of God. What is not the Word of God cannot be declared to be the Word of God by the church. If Scripture as the Word of God is in such doubt as to whether it is the Word of God or not and so needs the church to declare it to be such, then it is not the Word of God. To reverse the matter, the church cannot declare salt to be sugar or sugar to be salt. Sugar and salt are self-authenticating to the tongue and so is the Word of God to the human spirit. The later theologians designated this power of Scripture to authenticate itself by such Greek words as *autopistos* (credible within itself) or *aksiopistos* (worthy of belief by virtue of its own inherent worthiness).

Section 7: The Reformers returned to the canon of the Hebrew Testament with regard to the canon of the Old Testament

The historical details are as yet very obscure, but beginning with the third century before Christ, the Jewish Scriptures were translated into the Greek language in the city of Alexandria. This translation is known as the Septuagint, and the list of books it contains is known as the Alexandrian canon. There is no one single document that contains the Septuagint intact, but the Septuagint is formed by a compilation of different manuscripts. Because Greek was the *lingua franca* of the Roman Empire, the Septuagint functioned as the Old Testament for the Christian churches. When the Scriptures were translated into Latin forming the Old Italia versions, the translation was not made from the Hebrew text but from the Greek Septuagint. The translation into Latin included then the Alexandrian canon. There was such a proliferation of these translations into Latin with such embarrassing variations that Pope Damasus ordered Jerome to make a fresh translation.

Jerome knew that to do this task properly he had to translate from the Hebrew Testament, so he went to Palestine and lived there for twenty years learning Hebrew and translating the Old Testament into Latin. But when he studied the Hebrew Testament, he found that it did not contain all the books that were in the Alexandrian canon of the Septuagint. These extra books that he found are known in Protestant circles as the Apocrypha. Jerome suggested that these books be gathered together and put between the two Testaments as a unit indicating their secondary character. But this was not done, and the Latin Vulgate contains the Apocrypha as it occurs in the Septuagint.

In the tradition of the humanism abroad in the sixteenth century, Luther began to translate the Scriptures into German, using the original languages as the basis for his translation. When he left the Diet of Worms (April 1521), his friends pretended to capture him in order to protect his life and then carried him away to the Wartburg castle. There in a few short weeks he translated the Greek New Testament into German. Much later, when he started to translate the Old Testament as the leader of a team of translators working with the Hebrew text, he found out what Jerome had discovered. The Apocrypha was not in the Hebrew text used in the synagogues. He also discovered Jerome's advice that these books should be collected and put between the Testaments to indicate their secondary importance. This Luther did when he finished the translation of the Old Testament and presented the Luther Bible to the German people.

None of the three great divisions of the Reformation—Lutheran, Reformed, Anglican—recognized the Apocrypha as the Word of God. In the Anglican church it is retained as part of the Bible but is to be read only for edification. No doctrine may be constructed from the Apocrypha. The Apocrypha and the related Pseudepigrapha are valued by Protestants for their historical materials as well as their help in understanding the Hebrew mind before the birth of Christ. While not recognizing them as Scripture, they do not totally discard them.

The Jews throughout the world, the various branches of the Protestant church, and certainly contemporary evangelicals accept the Palestinian Jewish canon of the Old Testament in opposition to the Roman Catholic Alexandrian canon, although some scholars contest the concept of such an Alexandrian canon.

Section 8: The Reformers rejected the Roman Catholic doctrine of tradition

In Roman Catholic theology, as previously stated, Jesus Christ handed the revelation that came through him to his disciples as Tradition. This Tradition divides into two parts: the written which forms the New Testament and the oral which is perpetuated in the Roman Catholic church as tradition. This tradition has the same attributes of authority and infallibility that the New Testament has and is therefore a source of Roman Catholic doctrine. Whether something may be deduced solely from the tradition with no support at all from the New Testament is a problem debated within Catholicism but no concern of ours. Futhermore, some concessions of the priority of the New Testament over tradition have been made in recent times by Roman Catholic scholars, but again our interest is with Reformation times.

The Reformers rejected the concept of tradition on three grounds: (1) All that God intended the church to have of the revelation through Christ and his apostles he had written in the New Testament. It is the one and only Tradition. (2) Certain doctrines and practices supported by tradition in the Roman Catholic church are at variance with the clear teaching of the New Testament. (3) It is impossible actually to specify the borders of this tradition or its precise contents. What makes the historian so suspicious about tradition are the numbers of fantastic apocryphal legends that grew up around Christ and his apostles known as the New Testament Apocrypha.[3]

Much of the discussion of disputed doctrines involved discussions of the opinions of the church fathers as they would be the most likely to cast oral tradition into written form. If Calvin was not the most learned man of all Europe of his times in the knowledge of the Fathers, he was at least so competent in this knowledge that no Roman Catholic scholar dared debate him in public about the theology of the Fathers.[4]

The rejection of tradition led to the Reformation doctrine of *sola Scriptura*—only the canonical Scriptures are inspired and have authority in the church as the Word of God. Again, just as the Reformers rejected the inspiration of the Apocrypha but did not reject its historical worth, so they did not completely reject tradition. They had great respect for what was ancient in the church, especially in the Anglican and the Lutheran churches. Although the Fathers did not have the same place of authority among the Reformers as they did and still do have with Roman Catholic theologians, nonetheless the Reformers highly respected the views of the Fathers. Both Luther and Calvin were indebted to Augustine, a church father, more than any other source outside of sacred Scripture. However, to them the Holy Bible was the only Word of God. As valuable as other sources may be, they are not inspired and therefore not authoritative. And with the Reformers the contemporary evangelical says that *sola Scriptura* yet stands.

Section 9: The Reformers rejected the authority of the Fathers and the councils

The Fathers were the great bishops, teachers, and theologians in the church from the death of the apostles to Isidore of Seville (560–636). In Roman Catholic theology the opinions of the Fathers are binding when they agree in faith and morals. Peter Lombard (1100–60) collected the opinions of the Fathers into four books which he called *Sentences*. This was the basic textbook of theology for the theologians of the Middle Ages, and it is said that Thomas Aquinas could not have written his *Summa Theologica* without it.

In loyalty to their belief in *sola Scriptura*—only Scripture—the Reformers did not accept the authority given to the Fathers by the Roman Catholic church. As mentioned in the previous section, the Reformers thought very highly of the Fathers and depended much on Augustine. However, high veneration of the opinions of the Fathers and even an almost slavish dependence on Augustine is not the same thing as recognizing their common opinions as binding upon Christian theologians. The Fathers are especially valued in the Anglican church, and it was the Anglican interest in the Fathers which set it to systematically translate their writings into English (*The Ante-Nicene Christian Library* and *The Nicene and Post-Nicene Christian Fathers*).

According to the Roman Catholic church the decrees of an ecumenical council are infallible and binding on Catholic conscience. Here again the stance of the Reformers is consistent. The councils are not binding in their decrees. Part of the nineteenth article of the Thirty-nine Articles of Religion of the Anglican church reads: "As the Church of Jerusalem, Alexandria, and Antioch have erred; so also the Church of Rome hath erred, not only in their living and manner of Ceremonies, but also in matters of Faith." This is an implicit denial of papal and Roman Catholic claims. In article twenty-one the wording is more explicit, for the title is "Of the Authority of General Councils." It is affirmed that even lawfully gathered assemblies not guided by the Spirit or the Word of God may err, and as a matter of fact they have erred in matters regarding God. Anything such assemblies declare to be necessary for salvation which is not in harmony with Scripture has no strength or authority.

This generally expresses the opinions of the Reformers. It is true that Luther wanted to call a council rather than depend on the arbitration of the pope or debates with Roman Catholic theologians. But the pope would not concede to Luther and call a council, so eventually Luther did not recognize the official status of a council. On the other side of the ledger is the fact that all branches of the Reformation accepted some of the decisions of the early councils, especially the christological formulations.

Section 10: The Reformers rejected the Roman Catholic doctrine of the clarity of Scripture

The Scripture is a long book with a great diversity of literature and themes. It is broken in the middle by a body of pre-Christian revelation, the Old Testament, and a body of Christian revelation, the New Testament. In addition to this, it is an oriental book with flora, fauna, geography, peoples, customs, and languages foreign to the Western mind. How does the interpreter make sense of this strange and diverse book, and what is the unity in the midst of such great diversity? Is there a theme that binds it all together, or is it in the final analysis a hodgepodge of theologies? This is the problem of the clarity of Scripture.

The Roman Catholic church had its own version of the clarity of Scripture. Although its official pronouncement on the subject is in the Council of Trent which convened after the Reformation, the pronouncement nevertheless reflects the pre-Reformation belief of the Roman Catholic church. In the fourth session (1546) the council discussed Scripture, Tradition, and the interpretation of Scripture. With reference to the interpretation of Scripture, it claimed that the "mother Church" has the right to "judge of the true sense and interpretation of the holy Scriptures." That is to say, grace is given to the teaching magisterium of the Roman Catholic church to know the right meaning of Scripture and thus make Scripture clear. This is the formal theory of the clarity of Scripture in the Roman Catholic church. The material theory of the clarity of Scripture is that the system of doctrine taught in the church, especially the *de fide* teaching (that which all Catholics believe as part of saving faith, the so-called theological faith), is the true system of theology contained in Holy Scripture. In short, the Roman Catholic church makes the Scripture clear. It may also be inserted here that the four-fold method of biblical interpretation is also part of the Roman Catholic doctrine of the clarity of Scripture. This has been mentioned before as growing out of patristic interpretation and Augustine's three-fold system of biblical interpretation.

If the Reformers rejected the theory that the church has the grace or gift to make the Scriptures clear, then how are the Scriptures made clear? Perhaps the clearest break-through at this point is Luther's work, *The Bondage of the Will,* written in 1525 to rebut a previous very humanistic book by Erasmus—although it was anticipated in a remarkable way in Zwingli's *Of the Clarity and Certainty or Power of the Word of God.* In developing his theses Luther speaks of the external clarity and the internal clarity of Scripture and so gives the basic Protestant answer to the problem of the clarity of Scripture.

The external clarity of Scripture is its grammatical clarity. By the ordinary rules which govern the understanding of texts, especially the ancient texts, the Christian interpreter could understand the meaning of Scripture. Sometimes Luther calls this the literal sense of Scripture. If the ordinary principles of grammar could make sense out of Scripture, then a special gift of grace to the church to understand Scripture is not necessary.

But there is another factor to be considered. Scripture is also the Word of God. The Word of God is something spiritual and therefore can only be spiritually perceived or understood. Sinners cannot discern or understand or recognize spiritual truth. The internal clarity of Scripture is the work of the Holy Spirit within the believer, enabling him to spiritually understand the Word of God. There was to Luther, besides the internal and external clarity of Scripture, a thematic clarity of Scripture. That thematic clarity of Scripture is Jesus Christ. Jesus Christ is the unity, harmony, burden, and substance of Scripture.

Calvin's position is virtually identical to Luther's although he has the advantage of being more articulate since he comes later in history and can profit from Luther's advances. Calvin works out a very thorough doctrine of the Holy Spirit which centers in his doctrine of the witness of the Spirit in book one of the *Institutes of the Christian Religion* and in book three where he states that the benefits of Christ's salvation are bestowed upon believers by the secret operation of the Holy Spirit. As far as the thematic clarity of Scripture is concerned, Calvin affirmed that Christ is the mediator of all of God's revelations in both Testaments.

The Reformers also had the motto that "Scripture interprets Scripture." The word *Scripture* means two different things here. The idea is that the context of any part of Scripture is the total Scripture. Operationally it can be stated two ways: (1) No interpretation of a passage of Scripture may clash with the total teaching of Scripture; or (2) Where a passage of Scripture is obscure, it is to be understood or boxed in in light of the total teaching of the Scripture on the subject. The purpose of the motto is to show once again that the Protestant interpreter does not need to fall back upon the church at certain critical places in the interpretation of Scripture, for Scripture is complete in itself.

The Reformers' doctrine of the clarity of Scripture must be seen in light of the status of scholarship of the period. The scholasticism of the medieval scholars had reached a low point at the time of the Reformation. In the meantime another type of scholarship known as humanism emerged from the Renaissance. At the time of the Reformation the universities in Germany were divided. The old scholasticism prevailed at Tübingen, and it drove away Melanchthon who was exposed to the new humanism at Heidelberg. In turn, Luther was educated at Erfurt where the new humanistic scholarship prevailed. Calvin was also educated in the new humanistic scholarship, and his first published work was a very precocious bit of scholarship on a secular theme. It was an investigation of Seneca's *De Clementia* (1532). The greatest scholar in Europe using this new humanism was Erasmus although there are some who believe that the title belongs to Melanchthon.

This humanistic scholarship was concerned with the determination of the best texts of the Latin and Greek classics; with adequate Greek and Latin grammar lexicons; and with expert ability in these languages to read and translate these texts properly. This scholarship was also interested in establishing which texts were authentic and which were spurious. Calling their method philology, they included the entire critical apparatus of history, geographical details, and any other kind of information that would aid research.

It was this humanistic scholarship that lay behind the Reformers' theory of biblical interpretation and the way they approached the interpretation of Scripture. By virtue of this new humanistic scholarship Calvin was able to write the first scientific commentary on the Scriptures in the history of the Christian church.

The Reformers did include the work of the Spirit in their understanding of Scripture, and so the motto of the Reformation was "the Word and the Spirit."[5] As helpful as the humanistic scholarship was, it was not adequate for the total problem of the interpretation of Scripture and the clarity of Scripture.

Section 11: The Reformers taught justification by faith alone

That which made Martin Luther a Reformer and not merely a protestor was the intersection in his life of his personal spiritual struggle to find a real sense of peace and forgiveness with God and his exegetical studies as a professor in the university at Wittenberg.

As far as his spiritual struggle is concerned, none of the comforts or consolations of the Roman Catholic church gave him peace of heart. Even such a saintly man as Staupitz and some of the remarkable advice he gave Luther could not bring rest to Luther's mind. Erik Erikson's *Young Man Luther* is an attempt to understand Luther's struggle from the standpoint of psychoanalytic theory.

Luther approached the study of Scripture with the scholarship of the new humanism. During the Middle Ages the righteousness of God had stood for God's retributive judgment. The redeemed would receive mercy and the bliss of heaven, and unbelievers would be judged and sent to hell. Luther found, first in his study of the psalms and later in his study of Galatians and Romans, that righteousness was in some instances the possession of a believer. If Luther could feel that he possessed this righteousness, then his problem of guilt and the uneasiness he had with the wrath of God would be settled.

Scholars of Luther have argued extensively in attempting to defend the particular time when Luther's internal spiritual trek and his interpretation of Scripture intersected to give him his "evangelical experience." It is dated somewhere between 1514 and 1517. Germane to this is his story of his *Tower Experience*. This was recounted in his old age, and Luther scholars are not sure whether he is accurately recounting something he had never heretofore disclosed or whether it is an imaginative reconstruction of events by an elderly man. But it did happen, and it happened before Luther posted his theses in 1517.

The first significant deviation, then, from standard Roman Catholic theology was that righteousness was not only the retributive justice of God but something believers possessed.

The second was that righteousness was received by imputation, by God's verdict, and not by infusion as taught in Roman Catholic theology.

The third is contained in the word *alone*. Luther saw the Galatian heresy repeated in the Roman Catholic church. The Galatian heresy was the attempt to make the gospel a fusion of law and grace or more concretely to fuse circumcision from the Old Testament and faith in Christ in the New Testament. Paul said that such a syncretism was impossible. Luther saw the Roman Catholic church attempting to make a synthesis of ecclesiastically specified works and faith in Christ as the way of salvation. If the gospel is to be without the law, Luther believed it is also to be without ecclesiastical works.

The expression *apart from the law* (Rom. 3:21) meant justification by faith *alone*—the *alone* excluding the Mosaic law. So, too, with the Roman Catholic system. *By faith alone* meant justification apart from ecclesiastical works (or good works or works of love or so-called worthy acts of penance).

The fourth significant deviation is that the combination of sanctifying grace or infused grace of justification, regeneration, and sanctification is broken up by Luther into three separate though conjoined acts of God. Unless this is done, man's works become part of his salvation.

The fifth deviation led to a new interpretation of the priesthood of believers. Contrary to much common Christian opinion, the priesthood of believers was not originally that every soul has equal access to God or the concept of the competency of the soul. It meant that each believer was to be a priest to every other believer. It broke down the split of the church into the sacramentally ordained priest and the laity and made the entire church the people of God and a kingdom of priests. It was later in the history of theology that the priesthood of believers was understood to mean that each Christian is a priest and each Christian has equal access to God and each Christian can care for his own sins by personal confession.

Section 12: The Reformers reconstructed the doctrine of the church

The Roman Catholic church taught that Jesus founded a Divine Society with a hierarchy before he ascended to heaven. That Divine Society is none other than the Roman Catholic church. As a Divine Society it is a functional part of the plan of salvation: it is part of the inner mechanism of redemption. It is a hierarchy of pope, cardinal, bishop, priest, and deacon whose right it is to rule, which means the right to make laws and assess penalties. It is the duty of each Catholic layman to submit himself to the hierarchy as submission to Christ. It is also a priesthood in that the grace of Christ and the salvation of Christ are mediated by the priests through the sacraments.

By virtue of the sacraments the believer is saved (baptism), empowered to lead the Christian life (confirmation), forgiven if he sins so that he can continue in the Christian life (penance), and reinforced in grace (the mass). If he marries, he is given supernatural grace for the calling of husband or wife (matrimony), and when he is sick unto death, he is prepared for the world to come (extreme unction). The rules of the game are contained in the *Canon Law* so that as much guesswork as possible is removed from the relationship of believer and hierarchy. The Roman Catholic church is in the act of salvation itself. This church is indwelt by both Christ and the Spirit so that to obey the hierarchy is really to obey the Christ and the Spirit who inhabit the church. The church is not sinlessly perfect but is composed of forgiven sinners; nevertheless

the church as a whole is indefectable, and therefore separation from
the Roman Catholic church is the sin of schism.

The Reformers did not deny that the church is a divine institution.
Nor did they deny that local congregations were truly manifestations
of the one body of Christ. Nor did they deny the place of ministers
or sacraments. In their own way they could say that the church is
the mother of us all and that apart from the church there is no salvation. The amount of substantial ecclesiology taught by the Reformers
has been frequently underestimated, especially by ahistorical
evangelicals.[6]

The Reformers modulated the doctrine of the church in two
ways: (1) *The church is seen as an instrument of grace* and not a
dispenser of grace or a controller of grace. As Schleiermacher was
later to say, in Roman Catholic ecclesiology the believer relates himself to the church which in turn relates him to Christ, whereas in
Protestantism the believer is directly related to Christ who in turn
relates him to the church.

The essence of the Reformers' view of the church is congregationalism (not to be confused with the Congregational churches). This
means that the church is not a Divine Society, an international
organization, an institution with laws and penalties, or a body of
people governed by canon law. Rather the one universal church of
Christ, the body of Christ, the invisible church, is manifest in history
in the form of local congregations.

One of the best articles in the famous Kittel's *Theological Dictionary of the New Testament* is on the church and was written by
K. L. Schmidt.[7] There is no doubt left in my mind that the Reformers' congregational view of the church is more than supported
by this article. This congregationalism means that the larger structures
of the church (associations, synods, assemblies, conventions, meetings, and so on) are built up from and by local congregations, rather
than the reverse in which local congregations exist by virtue of the
Divine Society.

(2) The Reformers made the minister the minister of the Word
of God. One of the sacraments of the Roman Catholic church is
that of holy orders. By virtue of being ordained, a priest receives
power to forgive sin in the sacrament of penance and the power to
convert the bread and wine of the mass into the body and blood of
Christ. Furthermore, this is an indelible sacrament which means it
can never be effaced or lost and therefore can never be repeated. No

matter what happens to a priest morally or theologically, he retains this power until death even though the church has the right to restrain his use of it.

The Reformers stated that the dignity, specialty, and authority of the Protestant minister did not rest in his ordination as such but in the Word of God. That which the minister offers the people of God is the Word of God—in sermon, in sacrament, in teaching, and in counseling. Ordination is not a sacrament, and it is not indelible. A man may defect from the ministry or may resign from the ministry or may be deposed by the church.

The center of the Word of God is the gospel. It was the conviction of the Reformers (and we include in this term not only the two giants, Luther and Calvin, but the lesser known men such as Zwingli, Farel, Bucer, Vermigli, Melanchthon, Cranmer, and so on) that the sacraments should be limited to gospel sacraments. By this rule the seven sacraments of the Roman Catholic church were reduced to two—baptism and communion. To be a minister of the Word of God meant then also to be a minister of the sacraments for they are the "visible words of God." Sometimes an ordination certificate will state that the minister is ordained to the gospel ministry rather than to the ministry of the Word of God. This is done to emphasize that the Great Commission is the primary mission Christ gave to his church, and therefore the primary mission of the minister is to fulfil the Great Commission. To express this as the central concern of the minister, the ordination certificate specifies that the minister is ordained to the "gospel ministry."

We now have before us the theological differences between the Reformers and the Roman Catholic church. Although evangelicals have differences within their own household, they are almost in uniform agreement with the Reformers' theological stance. Just as the evangelical is more in harmony with the theology of the Western church than the Eastern, he is also far more in harmony with the theology of the Reformers than that of the Roman Catholic church.[8]

As previously mentioned, the Roman Catholic church has made some modifications of its theology, especially in the twentieth century. For example, Hans Küng attempts to show in his book *Justification* that the Reformers and the Council of Trent are not as far apart as presumed. There is an imputational element to justification. He has become more extreme in his recent book, *Infallible? An Inquiry,* in which he virtually agrees with the Reformers that only God is infallible and therefore the papacy and the council, while always within the banks of the truth, are not infallible in their pronouncements. Other Roman Catholic writers have said that whereas the Council of Trent had said that the written and oral tradition are of equal veneration that is not to say that they are of equal importance and so take a step or two in the direction of the Reformers. Or to admit that the Latin Vulgate has theological authority but not critical authority is to again concede some points to the Reformers. Such modifications suggest that the Roman Catholic church is tacitly admitting the correctness of some of the positions of the Reformers, so a current assessment of Roman Catholic and Protestant differences would differ materially from this historical assessment I have given.

NOTES

1. This legend is found in the New Testament apocryphal book, Acts of St. Peter.

2. Some think this is the Linus of 2 Tim. 4:21, but this cannot be proved. The basic evidence is that lists of bishops of Rome in patristic literature name Linus after Peter.

3. The definitive work is that translated by Montague R. James, *The Apocryphal New Testament* (New York: Oxford University Press, 1924).

4. Calvin's most sustained attack upon the theology of the Roman Catholic church is found in his discussion of the theology of the church in bk. 4 of *The Institutes of the Christian Religion,* ed. John T. MacNeil, trans. Ford Lewis Battle. *Library of Christian Classics,* vols. 20, 21 (Philadelphia: Westminster, 1960).

The heart of Luther's divergences from Roman Catholic theology may be found in his three great tracts of the year 1520: *To the Christian Nobility of the German Nation; The Babylonian Captivity;* and *The Freedom of the Christian Man.*

5. I have dealt extensively with the doctrine of the witness of the Spirit in my book, *The Witness of the Spirit* (Grand Rapids, Mich.: Wm. B. Eerdmans, 1960), attempting to show its Reformation origins and its relevancy for today.

6. Calvin's massive reconstruction of the doctrine of the church will be found in bk. 4 of the *Institutes.* For the Lutheran view of the church, consult the Book of Concord or the section on the church in H. Schmid, *The Doctrinal Theology of the Evangelical Lutheran Church,* trans. C. A. Hay and H. E. Jacobs (Minneapolis: Augsburg, 1961), part 4, chap. 3. For the Anglican Reformation, see Philip Hughes, *Theology of the*

English Reformers (Grand Rapids, Mich.: Wm. B. Eerdmans, 1965), chaps. 4–7.

7. K. L. Schmidt, *"Kaleō et al.," Theological Dictionary of the New Testament,* ed. G. Kittel and G. Friedrich (Grand Rapids, Mich.: Wm. B. Eerdmans, 1966–69), 3:487 ff.

8. For an interesting study of the present status of the key Reformers' beliefs, see W. D. Niven, *Reformation Principles after Four Centuries* (Glasgow: Pickering & Inglis, 1953).

Chapter Three

THE DIVIDED HOUSE
OF PROTESTANTISM

Section 13: The sacramental issue

If there was a dream that the Reformers would hold a common, united front against the Roman Catholic church, it was unrealistic.[1] From the Protestant standpoint, few things could be more desirable, but no such unity was in store. If there was a common front, it ended in 1529. What were the theological differences which broke the common front of the Reformation?

The first was the sacramental issue. At the Diet of Worms in April 1521, Luther refused to recant and deny his writings, and so the papal ban became effective but with the provision that he have safe journey back to Wittenberg. The actual beginning of the Reformation as a movement may be dated from that time, for as of then it was no longer a protest or a complaint within the Roman Catholic church. Luther's words were: "Hier stehe ich. Ich kan nicht anders. Gott helff mir—Here I stand. I cannot do otherwise. God help me."

Luther's career as a public Reformer (in contrast to the inner spiritual and theological Reformation that had been going on for some years) began when he nailed his ninety-five theses for debate on the door of the university cathedral, which served as the bulletin board for the university. By virtue of the printing press, these theses became published as well as translated and republished in most of the countries of Europe. The first reaction of the Roman Catholic church was to engage Luther in a series of debates. These famous debates occurred between 1517 and 1520.

While all of this was going on, Luther was being carefully followed and read by Zwingli in Zurich. As early as 1519, Reformation motifs were appearing in Zwingli's sermons. In 1523 the cathedral of the city of Zurich voted to adopt the Reformation platform suggested by Zwingli and a second front was opened.

The Reformation in Zurich spread to Geneva and Basel. Could the German and the Swiss Reformation move together in a common front? The first suggestion of a really serious difference appeared in the sacramental theologies of Luther and Zwingli. Luther apparently had a much stronger view of the sacraments than Zwingli. The differences were of such magnitude that a conference or colloquy was called at the city of Marburg for the year 1529. The German delegation was led by Luther, and the Swiss, by Zwingli.

As the debate progressed, it became apparent that the division was more serious than anticipated. Although Luther rejected much of the sacramentalism of the Roman Catholic church, he still insisted on his own version of the real presence of the body and blood of Christ in the Eucharist. While he admitted that *is* could be used metaphorically in such an expression as *I am the true vine* (John 15:1), Luther nevertheless felt that in the Eucharist the word *is* was an *is* of equation. *Hic est corpus meum!* "This is my body." That *is* could not be a metaphor.

On the contrary, Zwingli had read the exhaustive studies of a Dutch scholar on the use of the word *is* or the verb *to be* in the entire Bible. This study clearly demonstrated that the Scriptures are filled with phrases or sentences where *is* indicated a metaphor and could not be taken as an *is* of equation. Zwingli therefore felt that the entire linguistic usage of Scripture was in favor of the metaphorical meaning of *is* in *hic est corpus meum*.

The differences could not be reconciled, and when the companies parted, Luther remarked that the Reformed were of a different spirit than the Lutherans. He meant that the real difference was not about grammatical nuances and meticulous studies of the word *is*. Luther and the Lutherans saw creation as one system with redemption. If creation was part of the modality whereby God expressed and revealed himself as well as in his Word, then it was not superstitious or incredible that God should use earthly substances as part of the process of conveying grace to man.

Zwingli and the Reformed theologians saw the relationship between man and God as direct and immediate through the Holy Spirit. In this immediacy of grace, and in this direct mediation of the Spirit, substances were unnecessary.

To the Lutherans this was a faulty understanding of creation. In effect it made creation theologically neutral. This is what Luther meant when he said that the Reformed were of a different spirit than the Lutherans.

The sacramental issue then split the common front of the Reformation. At this point it was divided between Luther and the Lutheran churches and Zwingli and the Reformed churches.

Later on Calvin tried to bridge the sacramental gap between the Lutherans and the Reformed by introducing the presence of the Holy Spirit in the communion service. By doing this he would pull away from the barren symbolism or representationalism of Zwingli and move toward the Lutheran idea of real grace being present in the communion. But the Lutheran reply was that the Lord's Supper is the real presence of the body and blood of Christ and not of the Holy Spirit. Calvin's effort to heal the breach failed.

Other differences made the sacramental difference even more permanent. To Calvin the human nature of Christ, though truly joined to the divine nature, did not share in any way with the attributes of the divine nature. This has been known as the *extra-Calvinisticum*. On the other hand, the Lutheran theologians taught that the human nature could share in the divine attributes—the *infra-Lutheranum*. Because the human nature of Christ could share in the divine nature, the body and blood of Christ could be on all the Lutheran altars whenever communion was held. This is known as the ubiquity of the body of Christ. The body of Christ may be everywhere where there is a Lutheran altar, but it is not omnipresent like the divine nature of Christ.

Calvin's reply was that a body is made up of hands, feet, bones, and so on. One could not in good use of language call a piece of bread a body. The reply to this was that there is a regular body and a sacramental body. It is the sacramental body that is present at the Lord's Supper and not the literal, risen body of Christ. And so the Lutheran-Reformed division hardened.

Another significant division was over the relationship of law and gospel. Luther taught that God had two words for man: his word of judgment and wrath in the law, and his word of grace and forgiveness in the gospel. This is not a difference between the Old Testament and the New Testament but a fundamental distinction to be found in all of Scripture. The difference between law and gospel is fundamental to the manner in which Lutherans interpret Scripture and organize their theology.

Calvin and the Reformed church taught that the law was the moral seriousness of the gospel. Therefore law and gospel are not antithetic, but the law adds to the gospel the divine imperatives for a righteous Christian life. In modern times the issue has flared up all over again. Barth wrote a little pamphlet which he called *Gospel and Law*. In it he reaffirmed the historic Reformed position. The very reversal of the words—gospel and law, and not, law and gospel —was a theological goading of the Lutheran theologians. A number of Lutheran theologians responded to Barth's pamphlet indicating that not only did he not understand law and gospel correctly, but the very misunderstanding was symptomatic of further sickness in his theology. Barth's sturdiest opponent at this point has been the Swedish theologian, Gustaf Wingren (*Creation and Law*).

Section 14: The Anglican Reformation

Some of the lesser Reformers spent time in England, and some of the English scholars came to the continent. There was a constant flow of books and letters back and forth across the channel. Somehow the Reformation had to break out in England as it was sufficiently removed from Rome by distance, custom, and mentality not to be strongly bound to Rome like Italy or Spain.

The poorest version of the English Reformation is that Henry VIII broke the English church away from the pope because the pope would not give him a divorce (technically, an annulment). Even if this were the true explanation, Henry VIII could not have succeeded unless there was great popular support based on growing Protestant and Reformation ideas and feelings in England. However, we may date the Reformation's beginning in England from 11 July 1533, when the pope excommunicated Henry VIII. In the following year the church in England was reorganized and became the Church of England. The papacy did not speak officially about the validity of ordination in the Roman Catholic church. All of the priests and bishops as of 1533 had received Roman Catholic ordination. On 13 September 1896, Pope Leo XIII ended the ambiguity of Anglican ordination by declaring that Anglican ordination was no longer valid (*Apostolicae Curae*).

Was the Anglican Reformation separate from the others or of like faith and order? The evangelical part of the church claimed it for the Reformed wing of the Reformation, and to this day some books list the Anglican church as being within the Reformed movement. Archbishop Laud (1573–1645) was a strong and powerful leader of the church. He made the Church of England thoroughly Anglican so that it became truly a third unique branch of the Reformation. However, there remains yet within the Anglican church an evangelical wing which is more sympathetic with Reformed views than with Anglo-Catholic views.

No other country in post-Reformation times split into so many movements as England: Puritans, Brownians, Dissenters, Congregationalists, Presbyterians, Quakers, and eventually Methodists. In all of this theological confusion there was one common objective in mind: They wished to be as faithful to Holy Scripture as possible. They wanted to be biblical, orthodox, apostolic, and evangelical. No doubt in their zeal for distinctives they overread the Scriptures, but this must not distract from their intention to be truly biblical and orthodox.

The basic documents of the Anglican Reformation are the Book of Common Prayer and the Thirty-nine Articles of Religion. The Book of Common Prayer was an adaptation of the historic tradition of the church in England to the specific character of the Anglican church. The precise nature of the Thirty-nine Articles has been more difficult to establish. However, it is evident that these articles are heavily indebted to the Augsburg Confession (Lutheran) of 1530 which is taken as the most significant confessional statement of the entire Reformation. Furthermore, it was not the intention of the authors of the articles to innovate but to reproduce that which they thought was true, historic, and orthodox Christianity.[2]

Section 15: The Reformed division into Calvinists and Arminians

When Calvin died, he was succeeded in Geneva by Beza (1519–1605). In his *Tractationes Theologicae* (1570–82) and in his lectures, Beza defended a theological determinism which was much more severe than that of Calvin.

The students from Holland reacted to this stern determinism and began a movement of protest. They were called Remonstrants (derived from an obsolete verb which means "to present reasons against something"). The Calvinists in Holland did not approve of this protest and appointed Arminius (1560–1609) to rebut the Remonstrants. His Dutch name was Hermandszoon, but it was customary to Latinize one's name. Instead of curing the Remonstrants he caught the disease. Eventually the Remonstrants became known as Arminians although there is a small Remonstrant church in Holland today. (This is a very compressed discussion of a very mixed situation in Holland, for among other things it is still a matter of debate how much of an "Arminian" Arminius was.)

The followers of Arminius met in Gouda in 1610 and drew up their five articles as a theological counterpunch to Calvinism. The Calvinists replied by calling a synod at Dort or Dordrecht (1618–19).[3] Although the Canons of Dort are much longer than the Five Arminian Articles (1610), they have been traditionally summed up by the rubric of TULIP: T—total depravity; U—unconditional election; L—limited atonement; I—irresistible grace; P—perseverance of the saints.

If Arminianism had remained cooped up among the Remonstrants in Holland, the history of theology might have been very different. It spread to England, however, and among its converts was a student at Oxford named William Laud (1573–1645). Eventually Laud became one of the most powerful men in the Church of England, and besides initiating many ecclesiastical and liturgical reforms, he gave Anglican theology an Arminian impress. Whatever Reformed or Calvinistic elements that were in the Anglican church became a minority, and their viewpoint was championed in the evangelical church in the Church of England (which has been customarily divided into the high church, the broad church, and the evangelical church).

But the story does not end there, for in 1784 the Methodist church broke away from the Anglican church and took its Arminianism with it. Although it reduced the Thirty-nine Articles of Religion to Twenty-five Articles of Religion, it did not revert to Calvinism but retained the Arminianism of the Church of England. Still the story continues! The *pietism* or *enthusiasm* (technical words in theology indicating religious practices involving excited or ecstatic emotional states as characteristic of religious experiences)[4] characteristic of Methodism fed naturally into such later movements as Pentecostalism in all its various branches, holiness churches, and the Church of the Nazarene. All of these churches are essentially Arminian in their theology. Even the Baptists were originally divided in England, for

the General Baptists were Arminian in contrast to the Particular
Baptists who were Calvinistic.

It is unfortunate that as the history of Protestantism unfolds as a
movement it splinters more and more. Although there have been attempts to find a third way in the matter of the Calvinists and the
Arminians, none have won any significant following, and the breach
remains unmended. But on the positive side of the story, it cannot be
denied that both parties wanted to be biblical. Both parties wanted to
keep the major traditions of the Christian church. Neither wanted to
be an innovator of some new, unknown brand of Christianity. The
word *evangelical* is big enough to cover both parties, for in their
haste to defend their own opinions, they were prone to forget some
of the great central affirmations of the Christian faith that they held
in common. It may be that where they differ the difference might not
be either as great or as significant as the proponents of each view
make it out to be. God is always bigger than our theology, and the
Scripture more generous than our codifications of it. In fact, with
the advent of liberalism and then the various other movements of the
twentieth century, the Arminian-Calvinist controversy has cooled off
because both sides have had to face so many common foes.[5]

NOTES

1. An important source that parallels much of the material in this and
the following chapters is John Dillenberger and Claude Welch, *Protestant
Christianity: Interpreted through Its Development* (New York: Charles
Scribner's Sons, 1954).
2. For the whole story presented in a very readable manner, see
Stephen Neil, *Anglicanism*, rev. ed. (New Orleans, La.: Pelican, 1958).
3. For those interested in the texts themselves, consult Philip Schaff,
Creeds of Christendom (Grand Rapids, Mich.: Baker Book House,
1967), 3:545 ff.
4. The standard work on this subject is R. A. Knox, *Enthusiasm* (New
York: Oxford University Press, 1961). Bishop Butler was horrified with
Wesley's enthusiasm and branding it "a horrid thing" ordered Wesley
out of his diocese. The German equivalent of the word *enthusiasm* is
Schwärmerei, and Kant was as much disposed toward German enthusiasts
as Butler was toward the English enthusiasts.
5. I have not mentioned what has been called the fourth or radical
wing of the Reformation, namely, the Anabaptist groups. They are more
commonly known in America as Mennonites, but the movement originally

included the Zwickau Prophets, the Swiss Brethren, and the Hutterites. They were a very active group of people with some very distinctive ideas, but they produced no great theologian. Neither did they achieve any great new theological synthesis. For more information, see John C. Wenger, *Introduction to Theology* (Scottdale, Pa.: Herald Press, 1954). See also *Spiritual and Anabaptist Writers,* ed. George H. Williams and Angel M. Mergal (Philadelphia: Westminster, 1957).

Chapter Four

THE EVANGELICAL
HERITAGE IN
SCHOLASTIC ORTHODOXY

Section 16: The written heritage of the Reformation

When Pope Leo X heard of Luther's disturbing views and activities, he branded the situation as a quarrel among drunken priests. It was one of the greatest misjudgments of history! Before Luther and his fellow priests were through, entire countries were lost to the Roman Catholic church (for example, Denmark, Sweden, Norway, Finland, England, Scotland), large chunks of other countries had turned to Protestantism (Germany, Switzerland), and significant Protestant movements were started (France).

In addition to the ancient divisions of the church, there was now a new division—Protestantism. Ordinarily people think of Protestantism as a protest against Roman Catholicism. The etymology of the word does not quite bear this out. It is a word of affirmation not protestation, for the Reformation was not a protest that was similar to other prior protests which tried to purify or revive the Roman Catholic church. *Pro* means "before," and *testis* means "witness," so a Protestant means one who gives witness or makes his affirmation. True, the Reformation was a protest, but if it were only a protest, it would not have created a whole new form of Christian life. It was the affirmations of the Reformers that made the Reformation an enduring reality in Christendom, producing the phenomenon of Protestantism. It was an effort to affirm the true version of Christianity in opposition to that form of Christianity held in the Roman Catholic church which the Reformers considered a corrupt Christianity.

Our concern now is to turn to the literary heritage from which the contemporary evangelical draws his fundamental Protestant convictions.

The fountainhead of Protestant thought is the writings of the Reformers themselves. This body of materials is so enormous that one man spending a lifetime could still not master it all.

At this point we must be realistic and practical. Scholars are now translating into English the major writings of Martin Luther. This is known as the *American Edition of Luther's Works* and when completed will run to fifty-six volumes. The writings of Calvin in English are: *The Institutes of the Christian Religion* (to be read in the new translation in *The Library of Christian Classics*); *Letters* (three volumes); *Tracts* (three volumes); and his *Commentaries* (currently being retranslated). *The Library of Christian Classics* contains samples of Luther's and Calvin's writings as well as those writings of other important Reformers.[1]

The written heritage of the Anglican Reformation is contained in a library of books called *The Parker Society*.[2] Matthew Parker (1504–74) was one of the great Anglican Reformers who guided the church in England from its Catholic form through periods of stress and confusion to its Anglican form. In 1840 a group of men banded together as the Parker Society to publish the works of the great Anglican Reformers.[3]

A second source of great theological literature of the Reformation and post-Reformation periods is the great creedal statements that were written during this span of time. In English we have such resources as Philip Schaff's *Creeds of Christendom, Vol. III, Evangelical Creeds*; John H. Leith, *Creeds of the Churches;* and Henry Bettenson, *Documents of the Christian Church*. The United Presbyterian Church in the United States of America has published *The Book of Confessions* which contains the important Reformed creeds. The Lutherans have as their source book for creeds *The Book of Concord*.

The most impressive and important of the earliest confessions of the Reformation was the Augsburg Confession (1530). Although a number of men helped compose it, the main architect was Luther's closest friend, Melanchthon. Luther was not allowed entrance into Augsburg, so he stayed at a town a short distance away and received, corrected, and sent back daily reports of the progress of writing the creed. The purpose of the creed was an effort of Emperor Philip V to bring the Lutherans and Catholics together, for he needed common support for his battles with the Turks. Unfortunately, he was indifferent to the creed, so in 1531 Melanchthon wrote a lengthy defense of the confession known as the Apology of the Augsburg Confession. After a period of theological debate within the Lutheran church, the church issued a reconciling document of great importance known as the Formula of Concord (1580).

On the continent the standard Reformed confession was the Second Helvetic Confession (1566). (*Helvetia* is the Latin name for Switzerland.) In Germany, Ursinus and Olevianius produced the most famous of the Reformed catechisms—the Heidelberg Catechism (1536). Among English-speaking people the most famous creed is the Westminster Confession (1646). A copy of this creed crossed the ocean on the Mayflower and was the original theological document of New England theology. It has exerted enormous influence on the history of theology in America. In 1967 the United Presbyterian church published a new confession known as the Confession of 1967. In order to give a sense of historical continuity and to alleviate much of the criticism that would come if the Westminster Confession were dropped, the Presbyterian church published a book of confessions containing all the great confessions in the Reformed tradition.

The Anglican church has two fundamental documents—the Book of Common Prayer and the Thirty-nine Articles of Religion. The Book of Common Prayer not only contains liturgical materials but also the ordinal which has to do with the method of ordaining the clergy. Its purpose was to give the Anglican church its own special liturgies after it had broken with the Roman Catholic church. The other document is the Thirty-nine Articles of Religion (1563). The commentary most generally used for the interpretation of the articles is that of E. J. Bicknell (*A Theological Introduction to the Thirty-nine Articles,* originally published in 1919 but the present edition is one revised by Carpenter).

A third literary heritage of the evangelical is the great works of theology produced for the most part in the seventeenth century. This period has been called the period of Protestant scholastic orthodoxy. (1) It sought to consolidate the gains of the Reformation by systematizing theology around Protestant or Reformation principles. Because such works were considered standards or normative for subsequent generations, they are called *orthodox.* (2) It is *scholastic* because in the effort to systematize the gains of the Reformation huge volumes of theology were produced which went into great detail with many precise definitions or doctrinal mottos. These volumes of theology looked very much like the *Summas* (literally, a catalogue) of the scholastic theologians of the Middle Ages; hence, the label, scholastic.

Only a few ministers had access to all of this literature. To preserve this heritage for the Lutheran church, Heinrich Schmid went through the literature, lifted out the best paragraphs on the various doctrines, and published them in one volume that made the material manageable for the pastor (*The Doctrinal Theology of the Evangelical Lutheran Church*).[4] The same was done for the Reformed church by Heinrich Heppe (*Reformed Dogmatics Set Out and Illustrated from the Sources*).[5]

Unfortunately no such summary has been made of the English Reformers, but we do have Philip Hughes's *Theology of the English Reformers*.

This period of Protestant scholastic orthodoxy has been subject to sharp criticism. The first is that it represents a dated approach to theology. It is pre-Enlightenment theology—theology before scientific history, before scientific literary criticism, before the findings of modern science, and before the development of a truly critical philosophy.

The second criticism is that it represents a decay from the dynamism and openness of the Reformers. Luther and Calvin and other Reformers thought and wrote in an atmosphere of free creativity as they made a new way in Christendom. Kant's famous essay on the Enlightenment states that the enlightened man dared to think. Nietzsche said the opposite of truth was not error but cowardice—the failure of nerve to rethink and reevaluate all that was sacred in our Western tradition. In the realm of theology the Reformers did fulfill Kant's dictum to dare to think, and they did meet Nietzsche's criterion to think that which hitherto had been forbidden to be thought.

The charge against Protestant scholasticism is that it petrified, deadened, and stifled the free spirit of the Reformers. It was regress, not progress. A premium was set on correct thinking down to trivia and minutia, and the Reformers' dynamic faith, dependence on the Spirit, and courageous interaction with Scripture was sacked. Furthermore, a premium was put upon system or systematizing which is contrary to the openness of the world, the openness of God's grace, and the openness of the biblical revelation.

Judgments on this period contain a subjective element which creates a measure of distortion. What is to so many liberal and non-evangelical theologians a sad century for Christian theology is for confessional orthodox Lutheran and Reformed theologians the golden age of theology. The best brains of all of Europe had turned to Holy Scripture and theology to produce the greatest theological literature in the history of the Christian church.

The truth is certainly somewhere down the middle, but we wish to assess the positive gain of this period.

It was a period of great Protestant orthodoxy. The word *orthodoxy* may be used in many different ways depending on the context. Protestant orthodoxy generally refers to the great theological products of this period. One should not read this literature uncritically or removed from its historical perspective. This literature is to be read to discover the original, definitive expositions of what the Protestant version of the Christian faith is. Therefore no theologian, regardless of his persuasion, can afford to overlook this period.

The call to the evangelical to know this literature is even more important. Some of the basic roots of evangelical theology are to be found in the writings of these theologians. Regardless of their scholastic methodology, these orthodox theologians did pick up all the historical materials of real significance; they attempted to conserve and reproduce what the Reformers said; and they turned to the Scriptures with a new thoroughness and rigor of interpretation to find out as accurately as possible what Scripture taught on different theological topics.

Paul Tillich cannot be called an evangelical. At the time of his death he was recognized as the most outstanding theologian in America. His contemporaries classified him among the famous living theologians such as Brunner, Bultmann, and Barth. He achieved the rare distinction in Germany of lecturing on both the philosophical and theological faculties. In 1933 he migrated to America and taught with distinction at Union Theological Seminary. His opinions about Protestant orthodoxy should be then of great importance to any student of theology.

In his work, *A History of Christian Thought,* Tillich devotes a special paragraph in evaluation of this period of Protestant orthodoxy.

> Orthodox theology was and still is the solid basis of all later developments, whether these developments . . . were directed against Ortho-

doxy, or were attempts at restoration of it. Liberal theology to the present time has been dependent on the Orthodoxy against which it has fought. . . . Hence we should deal with this period in a much more serious way than is usually done in America. In Germany, and generally in European theological faculties . . . every student of theology was supposed to learn by heart the doctrines of at least one classical theologian of the post-Reformation period of Orthodoxy. . . . Even if we should forget about the Latin today, we should know these doctrines, because they form the classical system of Protestant thought. It is an unheard-of state of things when Protestant churches of today do not even know the classical expression of their own foundations in the dogmatics of orthodoxy. This means you cannot even understand people like Schleiermacher or Ritschl, American liberalism or Social Gospel theology, because you do not know what against which they were directed or on what they were dependent. All theology of today is dependent in some way on the classical systems of Orthodoxy.[6]

One of the most regrettable features of contemporary ahistorical evangelicalism is that it has no appreciation of this rich heritage, whereas a man like Tillich who rejects the doctrines has such a profound regard for it.

As a pastor, Karl Barth became famous in the theological world with his commentary on the Book of Romans which was first published in 1919. The University of Göttingen in northern Germany has a special chair endowed for Reformed theology by the Presbyterian Church in America since the regular university faculty is Lutheran. In view of Barth's commentary, he was invited to fill this post.

This put Barth in a dilemma. He had been out of school more than ten years working as a pastor, and he had not written a book on theology but rather a commentary. Yet when the semester began, he was expected to lecture on theology. Commenting on this predicament he wrote:

I shall never forget the spring vacation of 1924. I sat in my study at Göttingen faced with the task of giving lectures on dogmatics for the first time. No one can ever have been more plagued than I then was with the problem, could I do it? and how? [7]

Stating how much he was out of step with contemporary liberal theology in Germany, he then continues:

Then it was that, along with the parallel Lutheran work [that of H. Schmid] Heppe's volume [*Reformed Dogmatics Set Out and Illustrated from the Sources*] just published fell into my hands; out of date, dusty, unattractive, almost like a table of logarithms, dreary to read, stiff and eccentric on almost every page I opened; in form and content pretty adequately corresponding to what I, like so many others, had described to myself decades ago, as "the old orthodoxy." [8]

But the more Barth pondered Heppe's citations from the old orthodox theologians, the more he realized that here was the kind of theology that interested him and that led him directly back to the Reformers which were, in his opinion, far better than his religious liberal predecessors such as Ritschl and Schleiermacher. He then came to admire these older writers so much that he could say that he was amazed at their "long, peaceful breathing, the sterling quality, the relevant strictness, the superior style, the methods confident at least themselves, with which this 'orthodoxy' was wrought." [9] He continues that he has no intention of simply reviving these theologians or merely repeating them. But he said that he could not get on with his work until he had lingered at least on fundamentals at the historical segment of orthodoxy. He continues:

> Success can come only if we have previously learned to read the Reformers as the *Church's* teachers and, with them, Scripture as the document for the Church's existence and nature, and therefore to ask what Church science might be. That precisely may be learned, nay must be, from the early Orthodox men.[10]

If two of the leading theologians of the world at the time of their mature careers thought so much of Protestant orthodoxy that they considered it fundamental to learning any theology, then we had better reassess what we have thought of these theologians and not dismiss them flippantly as old-hat orthodoxy. Evangelical theologians in particular ought to become more familiar with this epoch of theology, for in it is to be found most of their roots. The bulk of the doctrines they hold as essential to a sound Christian theology were first formulated here in great detail. These theologians are closer to the Reformers than any other contemporary school of theology.

There is one really important connection in American theology with this tradition that is worthy of mention. One of these great Reformed orthodox theologians was Franciscus Terrettinus whose work *Institutio Theologiae elencticae* (1688 and 1700) was the textbook for many years at Princeton Seminary. Out of it came Charles Hodge's *Systematic Theology* and the work of his son, A. A. Hodge,

Outlines of Theology. No other works have been as influential in shaping the general contours of evangelical theology in America as the works of the Hodges. For example, the *Systematic Theology* of the Baptist theologian, Strong, is really built out of Hodge. Strong's three volumes are precisely and exactly outlined. The result has been that many smaller works on theology by a wide range of theologians of divergent traditions have used Strong as the basis for their books. In some instances it is very obvious that the writer is depending on Strong, and in others the dependence is discovered in a more disguised form but nevertheless is there. Thus, Charles Hodge's influence extends throughout much evangelical theology in America indirectly through the great dependence upon Strong and the polite plagiarizing of Strong.

Section 17: The evangelical heritage in scholastic Protestant orthodoxy

As already indicated evangelical theology shares in the essential affirmations of the Reformers. The second most important source of contemporary evangelical theology (perhaps mostly through mediating sources) is the theology of Protestant orthodoxy. It is important to attempt to specify what in particular has been inherited from that period.

The contemporary evangelical shares in the theological continuity of Protestant orthodoxy. All three of the major theological movements of the Reformation accepted explicitly or implicitly the great creeds of the patristic period of the Christian church: the Apostles' Creed, the Nicaea-Constantinople Creed, the Chalcedonian Creed, and the Athanasian Creed. Orthodox Protestantism did likewise, and therefore the contemporary evangelical is also heir to the substance of these creeds.

The evangelical does not think that these creeds are infallible. They are important because they reflect the struggle of the early church to come to a mature understanding of the person of Christ, the nature of the incarnation, and the doctrine of the Trinity.

Neither does the evangelical think that his accepting the creeds puts an end to further theological exposition of Christology and the Trinity. The creeds said the first great definitive word, but they did not say the last or final word. As G. C. Berkouwer has stated in his work, *The Person of Christ,* Chalcedon said some very important things, but to accept Chalcedon is not to end all further christological reflection.

Just two examples will suffice. In the twentieth century there have been exhaustive studies of the various titles or names of Christ (Warfield, Cullmann, Taylor, Hahn). This sort of research goes far beyond the broad strokes of Chalcedon. Philippians 2:7 says that in the incarnation Christ emptied himself. What does that verb (*kenoō*) mean? This has given rise to a number of kenotic Christologies. It also represents problems not touched upon by Chalcedon.

In contemporary theology it is vogue to brand these early creeds as the Hellenization of Christian theology. The authors used philosophical categories derived from Greek philosophy to express Christian theology. We are told that these creeds rest on a substance philosophy which is a betrayal of the biblical way of thinking and is out of step with the dynamic version of the cosmos as held in science today.

Most evangelicals are not impressed with this accusation which ultimately stems from Edwin Hatch's book *The Influence of Greek Ideas and Usages on the Christian Church* (1900) which in turn influenced the great church historian, Adolph von Harnack, who lent the great prestige of his name to Hatch's thesis.

The evangelical is not a Roman Catholic, and he does not accept these creeds as official church doctrine. If the evangelical felt that the creed betrayed the New Testament, he would be the first to give up the creed.

But the problem of the creeds is not one introduced by Greek philosophy or substance philosophy. The problems the creeds wrestled with are in the New Testament itself. When John said the Word was God (John 1:1), he raised the issue of the deity of Christ long before Nicaea. When he wrote that "the Word became flesh" (John 1:14), he raised the question of the incarnation long before Chalcedon. When Paul wrote "the grace of the Lord Jesus Christ and the love of God and the fellowship of the Holy Spirit be with you all" (2 Cor. 13:14), he raised the question of the Trinity before Augustine or the creed of Athanasius.

To say that the creeds are the product of the Hellenization of Christianity is not to settle the issues debated in the creeds. If we do not like the manner in which the early church settled the questions, then it is our burden to make more sense out of the New Testament with our formulations than it did with theirs. The important point is that the problems of the humanity of Christ, the deity of Christ, the incarnation of God in Christ, and the Trinity are raised in principle in the New Testament and did not originate with Greek substance philosophy or Hellenistic theologians.

When the evangelical reads the contemporary restatements of Christology and the Trinity, he finds that although they may be free of Hellenization and substance categories, they are far divorced from biblical truth (as in Tillich's Christology and doctrine of the Trinity). For all the alleged Hellenization and substance categories, the early creeds still come closer to the biblical witness than do the versions of many modern theologians.

A good portion of patristic theology was absorbed into medieval theology, and a good portion of medieval theology was taken over by the Reformers. A great deal of the materials of a standard Protestant orthodox work on theology can be found, for example, in Thomas Aquinas's *Summa Theologica*. Furthermore, the Reformers went back and read many of the Fathers and took some theological booty directly from them. As mentioned repeatedly before, next to Holy Scripture, Augustine was the greatest theological resource for both Luther and Calvin. Protestant orthodoxy thus shares in the best of patristic and medieval theology through the Reformers and through their own research. This deep historical rootage of orthodox Protestantism is then shared by evangelicals.

For example, Machen had no stomach for the word *fundamentalism*. Why, he asked, should the great historic faith of the church be called an *ism*? He considered it a cheap maneuver to label somebody a fundamentalist as if to indicate by that term some new brand of theology unheard of in the Christian church and so disguising all the denials of great cardinal doctrines of centuries of standing by the person making such a quip.

The modern evangelical agrees with Machen that he is no devotee of an *ism*. Evangelical theology has its roots deep in patristic, medieval, and Reformation thought. Not all that the Reformers said of worth has been perpetuated. The failure to translate Luther into English until the twentieth century has robbed many generations of his riches. The transmission of Calvin's *Institutes of the Christian Religion* has also been uneven, and even when available has been ignored. But orthodox Protestantism and its heir, contemporary evangelicalism, have tried to retain as much as possible of the good of Reformation theology.

The Reformation and post-Reformation creeds have been honored by Protestant orthodoxy and in turn passed on to evangelicalism. However, it can bear constant repetition that evangelicals are serious students of Holy Scripture, and all of these historical materials are assessed from the stance of detailed biblical interpretation.

We have already indicated the importance of Terrettinus on the Princeton school of theology [11] and the Westminster Confession on American theology, and in turn, on the evangelical theology in America. This drives another nail in the board to show the historical linkage and continuity of contemporary evangelical theology with historical theology.

The evangelical shares with Protestant orthodoxy the passion to be biblical. One cannot read these orthodox theologians without sensing their great devotion to Holy Scripture—to the *sola Scriptura* of the Reformers. They had a passion to write only a biblical theology. Unfortunately they did not completely succeed, but even this failure must not cause us to lose sight of the star they had set their sights on.

Although the Reformers rejected Aristotelian philosophy because it intruded so much in Roman Catholic scholastic theology, the children of the Reformers brought Aristotle back into theology. This diluted the efforts of the orthodox theologians to be really biblical.

Biblical theology, as we know it today, did not exist at that time. Nor did the theologians have all the resources that contemporary biblical scholars have. Regardless of such limitations, they did have a passion to be biblical. Their goal was stated later by Chillingworth (but this famous saying of Chillingworth must be seen in its context, otherwise it suggests a bald bibliolatry): "The Bible, I say, the Bible only, is the religion of Protestants." [12]

Contemporary evangelical theology wishes to share in this passion to be biblical, but it stands in a much better position to do so than did the orthodox theologians. Evangelical scholars have today the vast riches of tools for biblical research which enable them to write a better biblical theology.[13]

All sorts of charges have been made against the view of Scripture held by these orthodox Protestants. They so exalted the Bible, we are told, that it became a paper pope. They so venerated Scripture that they were guilty of bibliolatry. They were so defensive about Scripture that they took an obscurantistic view toward biblical criticism and modern science. They held a dictation theory of inspiration or a mechanical view of inspiration. They materialized revelation by affirming that it was preserved in a book. Scripture was the source of all sorts of theological propositions, and theology was but the systematizing and arranging of propositions. They were accused of rationalism in the manner in which they sought to defend the inspiration of Scripture. They substituted the letter of Scripture for the work of the Spirit, breaking down the Reformation motto of "the Word and the Spirit." They had a flat view of the Bible in which all assertions were on the same level of inspiration and authority. There were no trivia in Scripture as God would not inspire trivia. To some, even the vowel points of the Hebrew text were inspired—called "pricks" in those days—which we now know were late additions to the Hebrew text.

There is truth in some of these charges. These men did write before all the critical developments of the Enlightenment. But certain things may be said in their defense:

(1) In his work, *The Inspiration of Scripture: A Study of the Seventeenth Century Lutheran Dogmaticians,* Robert Preus has shown that many objections to the views of Scripture of these men are off target or simply not true. He documents how these men were more intelligent and more informed than the doctrinaire ideas or stereotyped pictures of this period have suggested.

(2) In his work, *The Christian Faith (Die christliche Glaube,* untranslated as yet), Werner Elert, one of the great Luther and Lutheran scholars of this century, claims that the Reformers were such spiritual giants that their insights into the meaning of the New Testament is better than the modern exegetes with all their scholarly training and tools. Orthodox Protestants are heirs of these insights into the New Testament, and the scholastic and at times pedantic way of writing should not obscure what has been inherited from the Reformers.

(3) It is clear from reading the works of both Schmid and Heppe that Protestant orthodoxy did retain the password of the Reformers —the Word and the Spirit. They did not drop the doctrine of the witness of the Spirit from their theology. If anybody either dropped it or miscalculated its significance, it has been recent fundamentalism. For the dualism of the Reformers' the Word and the Spirit they have substituted the monism of the Word. Christianity, according to the fundamentalists, is borne along solely by one proposed aspect of the perfectability of Holy Scripture, namely, its inerrancy. Whatever errors Protestant orthodoxy might have made, one of them was not to

drop the Holy Spirit out of the understanding of revelation, inspiration, and Holy Scripture.

Evangelical theology that knows its parentage wants also to retain the Word and the Spirit. It wants to put side by side with the divine inspiration of Scripture the divine witness of the Holy Spirit. It wants the biblical view as to how the Bible is to be believed. Furthermore, it wants the service of the best of modern biblical scholarship, and therefore does not want to retreat to obscurantism—the refusal to interact with modern learning whether of science, historical matters, or criticism.

Evangelical theology shares with Protestant orthodoxy the goal of precision in theology. The Protestant orthodox theologians apparently worked with the assumption that one system or schema of theology was beneath all the diversity of Scripture. It was the function of theology to root this out and to state it in some orderly or systematic fashion. Furthermore, each doctrine of this system was to be stated as precisely as possible. Not only was the statement to express exactly as possible the teaching of Scripture, but it was also to exclude error and heresy. Although Lutherans and Reformed theologians differed on the degree of correlation and systematization, they both worked toward the ideal of presenting as accurately as possible the biblical doctrines and their interconnections.

The evangelical does not fault this goal. Standards of truth, precision of statement, and accurate reflection of biblical teachings are commendable goals. Much modern theology is very critical of an attempt to achieve a system, or to state doctrines with precision, or to be guided by some degree of coherence. To the contrary, the evangelical wants as much truth, consistency, and precision as is possible under the circumstances. Why should theologians have less rigorous standards than scientists as far as rigor may be applied to theology?

The evangelical knows the limitations of the program of Protestant orthodoxy. For example, there is mystery in Christian theology (1 Tim. 3:16). It comes as a surprise that such a competent philosopher as I. T. Ramsey [14] should miss the point made by Michael Foster in his book, *Mystery and Philosophy.*

The evangelical does know the limits of consistency or systematization in theology. There are depths in the knowledge of God like an endless series of Chinese boxes within each other. Divine truth is like a light that penetrates the ocean, but the deeper it goes the dimmer it becomes until it vanishes. This is no attempt to escape rigor of thought but the intelligent recognition that the very idea of an infinite and transcendent God sets a limit to human thought in comprehending such a God.

Furthermore, the evangelical knows that theological concepts are complex and their relationships difficult to mark out clearly. No reflective evangelical claims to be able to correlate perfectly divine sovereignty and human freedom or the infinity of God and the incarnation or the unity and diversity in the Trinity or the personal and corporate nature of sin.

With Luther, the evangelical believes we must settle for a theology of the cross. With Kierkegaard, he believes the Hegelian claim to the System is grandiose beyond human powers.

Certainly the opposite is not the desire of theologians either, namely, a mere listing of doctrines. Reflective theological thought demands some correlating. The evangelical wants consistency as far as the biblical materials allow.

Further, the evangelical knows that new information is always forthcoming whether it be a scrap of papyrus from Egypt or something as dramatic as the Dead Sea Scrolls. This means that exegesis is always in some state of flux, and, therefore, theology built on exegesis must share the same degree of flux. We never know when new information will call for a new interpretation of a word or a verse or a passage.

The evangelical also knows that his own language is in a state of change. Modern linguistic studies reveal that all languages are in a state of shifting. Certain factors tend to slow the process down and others to speed it up. This means that theological concepts or words adequate for one period of time lose precision or meaning for a later period of time. The informed evangelical knows that language is at best an imperfect tool of expression and that theology must suffer the imperfections of language.

As much as the evangelical wants consistency and precision, he knows the limitations under which all human thought labors. He cannot have an ideal in theology that the realities of language will not justify. But he wants as much clarity as he can get under the circumstances; as much precision as he can get; and as much consistency as he can get.

To sum up, the modern evangelical is the distant heir of Protestant orthodoxy. His desire is to preserve the best of this tradition and add all the modern correctives necessary.

NOTES

1. Volumes 14–26 deal with Reformation literature.
2. One hundred fifty-six volumes being republished by London Publications in association with Johnson Reprint Corporation.
3. Volume 26 of the *Library of Christian Classics* is devoted to the English Reformers.
4. Heinrich Schmid, *The Doctrinal Theology of the Evangelical Lutheran Church,* trans. C. A. Hay and H. E. Jacobs (Minneapolis: Augsburg, 1961).
5. Heinrich Heppe, *Reformed Dogmatics Set Out and Illustrated from the Sources* (London: Allen & Unwin, 1950).
6. Paul Tillich, *A History of Christian Thought,* ed. Carl E. Braaten (New York: Harper & Row, 1968), pp. 276–77.
7. From Barth's preface to Heppe, *Reformed Dogmatics,* p. v.
8. Ibid., p. v.
9. Ibid., p. vi.
10. Ibid., Italics are Barth's.
11. It is the thesis of E. R. Sandeen, *The Origins of Fundamentalism,* that American fundamentalism is a synthesis of the theology of the old Princeton school and Darby dispensationalism.
12. William Chillingworth, *The Religion of Protestants* (London: Bell & Daldy, 1870), p. 463.
13. Hans Conzelmann makes the distinction between the use of the Bible in theology as in previous centuries and the recent idea of biblical theology as a specialized discipline within theology. See Conzelmann, *An Outline of the Theology of the New Testament,* trans. John Bowden (New York: Harper & Row, 1969), p. 3.
14. I. T. Ramsey, "Religion and Science: A Philosopher's Approach," *New Essays on Religious Language,* ed. Dallas High (New York: Oxford University Press, 1969), pp. 36 ff.

Chapter Five

THE MORTAL WOUND
TO ORTHODOX PROTESTANTISM
BY THE ENLIGHTENMENT

Section 18: The characteristics of the Enlightenment

Revelation 13 describes a beast with seven heads who arises from the sea. One of the heads has a mortal wound. This indicates the kind of wound inflicted on an animal to slaughter it, but the miracle is that the beast is not dead. Protestant orthodoxy received a mortal wound by the Enlightenment. But orthodoxy was not killed or slain; it did manage to survive. Nevertheless, the mortal wound inflicted by the Enlightenment on Protestant orthodoxy was a staggering one and from which there has never been a full recovery.

The term *Enlightenment* is one of those large, inflated concepts like humanism or the Renaissance or liberalism that defies a precise definition. Writers on the subject differ greatly as to the time of its origin, the time of its—are we still in it?—end, and what does or does not belong to it.[1]

The word *enlightenment* comes from the German word *Aufklärung* (French, *l'illumination*). It means that period in modern history when the educated or intelligentsia or *literati* (or as the French called them, *les philosophes,* intending much more than just philosophers but all learned men) turned their backs on the authority of antiquity and turned to trust their own powers. It repudiated the authority of the past or of tradition and affirmed modern man's power to find the truth for himself. It meant that modern philosophy was better than ancient philosophy and that modern science was better than Greek science. It meant that the supreme intellectual vice was dogmatism and the supreme intellectual virtue was tolerance. Heribert Raab claims that "the Enlightenment denotes the most revolutionary of all movements which the Occident has undergone in its course of history." [2]

Our concern with the Enlightenment is with those aspects which impinged on Christian theology. The following are some of those factors:

(1) The Enlightenment was a period when historical science matured and which produced as a by-product historical skepticism. There was real justification for this. So much supposed history and supposed reliable documents turned out to be fictitious.

(2) It was a period in which literary criticism was the subject of intense occupation, particularly criticism of the documents coming from the Middle Ages and classical antiquity. Here literary criticism and historical research overlapped, but both found out the same thing, namely, that a great number of trusted documents were spurious or forgeries or in error in many of their assertions of facts and history.

Gilbert Highet's *The Classical Tradition* shows how the critical literary researches and studies made at the time of the Enlightenment spilled over into the faculties of theology and created there what eventually was known as higher criticism.

(3) It was a period of the enthronement of reason. When Descartes started modern philosophy with a repudiation of traditional scholastic methodology and in imitation of the new mathematics and science, he put a premium upon the ability of human reason to find its own way. From England came Deism which affirmed that God had given every man reason not only to guide him in life and philosophy but also in religion. Existing prior to days of psychological testing, the Deists unwittingly presumed reason was a constant factor in all normal, adult people. Then from Germany came Kant with his three critiques, each one of which was a specialized function of *Vernunft*—reason. Reason was the arbiter of all things religious as well as philosophical, and in this Kant joined hands with the Deists.

(4) It was a period of the sciences. Although physics and astronomy came to early theoretical formulation with Newton, the other sciences were slowly on the move. The various advances of the eighteenth century prepared the ground for a scientific explosion in the nineteenth century. Chemistry, geology, biology, sociology, and anthropology—to name but the chief ones—received their theoretical

foundations which enabled them to move toward their more mature status in the twentieth century.

(5) It was a period of general religious skepticism. Pressure came from all sides to attack the foundations of Christianity—Protestant or Catholic, and religion in general, Jewish or Moslem. As Peter Gay suggests, many did turn to neopaganism during the Enlightenment, but some retained some form of religion. It was Kant who undermined the apologetics for orthodox Christianity, but he reinstated belief in moral law, freedom, immortality, and God in his *Critique of Practical Reason.* Such a violent repudiator of historic Christianity as Voltaire was nevertheless a Deist. The important matter here is the enormous reduction of the doctrines of traditional Christianity and the limitation of religion to belief in God and a moral order.

(6) It was a period of toleration. The classical debate of the period was between the dramatist Lessing and the strong, hard-shelled Lutheran leader in the city of Hamburg, Goeze. Much of what Lessing said against orthodox Protestantism must be seen in terms of this violent controversy between him and Goeze. Lessing expressed his idea of toleration in his play, *Nathan the Wise,* in which a devout Jew is the hero. But, as some interpreters affirm, Nathan is more the mouthpiece of Lessing. In either case it is not a Christian who is the leading character.

But the most telling part of *Nathan the Wise* is not that Nathan, a Jew and not a Lutheran, is the hero—for Lessing fought bitterly with the vigorous Lutheran apologist, dogmatician, and ecclesiastic of Hamburg, Chief Pastor Goeze—but the story of the ring (act 3, scene 7). A man has a ring that has the wonderful power of making the man who wears it loved of God and of men. It was the duty of the man to hand it on to his son. In the sequence of handing it on, one man has three sons. He loves each son equally dearly, and it is impossible for him to decide to which son to give the ring. So he has two perfect imitations made and gives each son a ring. The sons then get racked up over who has the original, but the imitations are so perfect that it is impossible to decide which is the original. Then Nathan makes the point to Saladin, to whom he is telling the story, that it is the attitude of the wearer which makes the ring work and not any magical property in the ring. So if each son acts as if he has the genuine ring, the ring will bless him and he will be loved of God and man.

Of course, the ring stands for the true religion. And Lessing, speaking through Nathan, expresses his religious toleration: "Possibly the father wished to tolerate no longer in his house the tyranny of just one ring" (that is, the imperious claim that one and only one religion is true). Rather, continues Lessing through Nathan, "Let each strive to match the rest in bringing to the fore the magic of the opal in his ring."

(7) It was a period of humanitarianism. The so-called eternal values of heaven as taught in orthodox Christianity were replaced by here-and-now values. *This* life was *the* life. The idea that man was to suffer, bear the brunt of disease and disaster, and carry his cross was first repudiated by Spinoza in his *Ethics*. Furthermore, it was Spinoza who taught that man ought to take a strong life-affirming attitude toward *this* life. These ideals of Spinoza became firm convictions of most of the intelligentsia of Europe during the Enlightenment.

(8) Finally, Enlightenment meant the maturity of man. In Lessing's famous work *The Education of the Human Race* (1780) he said that man passes through the same stages as an infant does as it grows to adulthood. Mankind is now in the age of adulthood and does not need typical religious supports. In Kant's famous definition of the Enlightenment, *What Is Enlightenment?*, he too declared man was now mature. Man had come of age. He ought to dare to think for himself! The crutches of antiquity were gone. Later on Comte was to say something similar when he stated that mankind went through three states of explanation: first, the universe was explained religiously; then when religion failed, man explained things metaphysically or philosophically; but now that science has and is come of age, man is to explain things scientifically.

Section 19: The specific attacks on Protestant orthodoxy

Christianity had not gone unchallenged during the Middle Ages and the beginning of the modern period. But it was the Enlightenment that broke the back of Protestant orthodoxy as the official belief of Western man, especially among the philosophers, intellectuals, intelligentsia, educators, scholars, professors, and the vast majority of theologians.

It did not extinguish orthodoxy, but it removed it from its central place as the system of thought that unified culture and life. There have been strong orthodox revivals since the Enlightenment, and in our day Billy Graham has spoken to more people than any other preacher or evangelist in history. But nonetheless Protestant orthodoxy has never regained the place it once held in Europe and America. Protestant orthodoxy and evangelicalism are no longer unique options among many and are no longer the presuppositions of our culture. No doubt Christian elements, hardly recognized, still form the backdrop of our civilization, but in no sense are these elements vigorously asserted in their original orthodox version. This moving of Protestant orthodoxy out of the center of cultural life in Europe and America has been the most important impact of the Enlightenment.

This rejection of Protestant orthodoxy has also manifested itself in specifics, and we turn now to those specifics:

(1) With the growth of scientific history, biblical history has been subjected to severe critical treatment. Because an event is recorded in Scripture is no longer held as proof of its occurrence. The rule apparently is that all biblical history is suspect until proved otherwise by archeological research and/or documentary evidence.

(2) Literary criticism of the classics was carried over to the literary criticism of Scripture. Skeptical opinions about the integrity of the Old Testament go back at least to Spinoza, and Lessing stirred up a hornets' nest by publishing Reimarus's (1694–1768) skeptical opinions about the historical integrity of the Gospels under the title of *Wolfenbüttel Fragments* (1774–78). There is a long story about the radical criticism of both the Old and New Testaments, but the important point is that it was the developments in the Enlightenment that gave such studies an enormous impetus.

(3) Whereas pre-Enlightenment Christian man read the Scriptures not only for theology but for facts and science of all kinds, the man of the Enlightenment substituted science for Scripture. It was now considered the indisputable prerogative of the astronomer, the physicist, the biologist, and the geologist to inform man of the origin of the universe, the mode of its functioning, and its facts.

(4) With the growth of modern philosophy, modern science, and learning in general, the supernatural became more and more suspect until it was ruled out. The universe was governed by immanent laws which were never interrupted or suspended or contradicted by the supernatural or miraculous. Whatever version of Christianity was to survive the Enlightenment, it would have to be a Christianity denuded of the supernatural.

(5) Reason and philosophy replaced divine revelation. What there was to know of significance, man could learn by the powers of his own reason. Deism had already said religion that did not conform to reason was not proper to be believed. The Enlightenment drove this position further and deeper. The mysterious, the mystical, the paradoxical, and the transcendental were all excised from religion.

(6) The doctrines of original sin and human depravity were vigorously rejected. The dour-and-sour view of man was contrary to man's nobility and the worthiness of the joys, pleasures, satisfactions, and artistic creations of this world. There was a return to the pagan rather than the Christian view of life, for the former was a robust affirmation of this life and its values whereas the latter was too negative, too world-denying, too depreciatory of man's achievements, too preoccupied with sin, salvation, and heaven. If not stated in so many words, the perfectability of man and the coming of a utopia were implicit in the presuppositions of the Enlightenment.[3]

(7) The Christian explanation of evil was vigorously rejected. The prevailing explanation of the Christian understanding of the origin of evil was that of Leibniz in his *Theodicy*. With great acuteness he developed his thesis that this is "the best of all possible worlds." It was supremely Voltaire who in his novel, *Candide,* with biting sarcasm, irony, and humor demolished Leibniz as far as the intellectuals were concerned.

(8) Religion was most offensive in its concept of dogma. As Cassirer states, "dogma is the most dreaded foe of knowledge [for the Enlightenment]." [4] This spelled the end of a Christian dogmatics as far as the Enlightenment was concerned.

(9) At this time the ethical criticism of Scripture begins. The slaughter of the Amalekites, the imprecatory psalms, and the drowning of the pigs (Matt. 8:30 ff.) were the kinds of biblical materials judged to be unethical. Some verses were especially offensive: "Happy shall he be who takes your little ones and dashes them against the rock" (Ps. 137:9); and the passage which describes two she-bears who killed forty-two boys (2 Kings 2:23–25).

In a sense the Enlightenment came to its clearest manifestation in Hegel. Hegel constructed a pyramid of the cultural elements in a civilization. Philosophy was at the top, followed by religion and art. What philosophy said literally, religion said symbolically. The competence of man's reason to speak literally of reality whereas religion could only speak symbolically and hence must by necessity be lower than philosophy in the scale of importance reveals clearer than anything else the heartbeat and the genius of the Enlightenment.

Section 20: An evangelical assessment of the Enlightenment

If the first great devastating blow against the Christian church was the success of the Moslem conquests, the second was the Enlightenment. Protestant orthodoxy never regained its status in Western culture after the blows of the Enlightenment. But as serious an attack as it was on Christianity, the evangelical cannot ignore it. Much of the scholarship that the modern evangelical uses he has inherited from the Enlightenment.

If a difference can be made between a fundamentalist and an evangelical, it can be made at this point. Fundamentalism attempts to shield itself from the Enlightenment. It attempts to do its theological and biblical tasks as if the Enlightenment had never happened. On the other hand, the evangelical believes that the Enlightenment cannot be undone. He must use the valuable tools of research developed during the Enlightenment, and he cannot ignore the entire change of the intellectual climate of Europe and America that the Enlightenment produced. The evangelical must come to terms with the Enlightenment in the following ways:

(1) The evangelical must come to terms with scientific history. He must know historiography (the rules for the writing of history) and possess a critical understanding of the nature of historical science. The evangelical is not so naïve as to believe that all historians see history the same way. Historians too have their denominations. But there are some hard-core premises held by all historians, and there is a general consensus concerning what is good writing of history and what is untrustworthy writing of history.

The evangelical believes in the bodily resurrection of Christ. He knows that this belief raises serious historical questions. He knows that theologians are as much divided about the relationship of biblical history to world history as they are divided about the nature of historical science. Bultmann, Barth, Cullmann, Pannenberg, and Moltmann each have their own method of relating biblical history to world history. The evangelical must have enough historical and theological sophistication to explain why and how he believes in the resurrection of Christ. The Enlightenment with its critical view of history demands this from him.

(2) The contemporary evangelical cannot ignore science as he holds to his faith in the supernatural elements in Scripture. Here again he must know something of the scientific method, the philosophy of science, and the nature of scientific knowledge. He must know something about verification and falsification, induction and probability, and the prescientific presuppositions which make science possible. Just as van Harvey has shown the historical problems of faith in Scripture in his work, *The Historian and the Believer,* the evangelical should know what problems modern science poses to his belief in the supernatural in Scripture. When he believes the supernatural, he must show that he has the theological and scientific sophistication to believe it responsibly. The development of the sciences in the period of the Enlightenment summons him to this responsibility.

(3) The contemporary evangelical cannot ignore biblical criticism. Contrary to the opinion of many evangelicals of the nineteenth century, biblical criticism was not a current fever that would pass away. Biblical criticism is here to stay, and the only response an evangelical can have toward it is to try to respond to it creatively. In a most critical chapter of his book, Thielicke argues that the real motivation for biblical criticism is theological. It is not an effort to be destructive or judgmental of Scripture. To the contrary! God honors our intelligence, and therefore he asks us to establish the pedigree of his Word.[5]

(4) The evangelical must follow the standards of research and scholarship established by the Enlightenment. There is a difference between *reason* and *reasoning.* The evangelical does not enthrone reason in his mind but God and his truth. Reasoning is the responsible way of arriving at conclusions. Reasoning is research and scholarship. The evangelical has no alternative to reasoning when it comes to principles of research or methodology of research.

The evangelical knows that scholars differ and that scholars differ in their reasoning. He also knows that there is no canonized reasoning. However, in spite of personal differences and presuppostions, there are some criteria of scholarship and some standards of reasoning which differentiate real scholarship from mere opinion or shoddy guess-work. So even while recognizing that reasoning itself is not capable of absolute definition, nonetheless the evangelical knows that to make his work acceptable to a community of scholars he must do his reasoning in a responsible way. The Enlightenment has demanded that tradition, custom, and hearsay be subjected to reasoning, and the evangelical is obligated to take heed.

(5) The evangelical must take seriously the possibility of false cultural assumptions infiltrating his theology.

Every theologian works in a climate of opinion or in a cultural atmosphere. Sometimes that which operates most powerfully in a man's thinking is that of which he is the least aware.

The doctrine of hell offers a prime example. When men of Western culture believed every soul to be responsible before God for every moral decision and that every right decision was to be rewarded and every wrong decision to be punished, preaching about hell was not considered offensive. Other factors too may have also made the preaching of hell unoffensive, for even in Greek and other religions was the idea that this life was the probationary period for a life to come in which we would be rewarded or punished.

Since Kant and the Enlightenment, religion has been interpreted more and more as equivalent to ethics, and the concept of God has been sentimentalized (that is, God's wrath and holiness have been eliminated or diluted by reinterpretation). Under such assumptions the doctrine of hell seems out of place, and hence preaching on hell is considered distasteful today.

Cultural assumptions that have crept into at least popular theology can at times be easily spotted. The strong distinction between body and soul that comes across in much evangelical preaching is Platonic rather than biblical. The neat division of man into body, soul, and spirit is more Neoplatonism than scriptural psychology. The concept of causation used in preaching is frequently causation as understood in the nineteenth century and not as understood in contemporary science. In theories of the atonement it can be shown how much the cultural atmosphere of the theologian determined the kind of theory of atonement he propounded.

The Enlightenment helped men see that they were children of their cultures. If a cultural atmosphere helped shape the science and philosophy of a period, it certainly helped shape the theology of the period. Evangelicals must then be alerted by the Enlightenment to see what possible cultural elements have entered their theology and distorted it from its original biblical base.

(6) Evangelicals must respond to the claim of the Enlightenment

that the Christian faith must be restated for each generation if it is to communicate with that generation.

Religious liberalism had the right inspiration but the wrong solution. Its inspiration was that the Christian faith had to be so rewritten that it would make contact with the mentality of the man of the Enlightenment. Its solution of recasting the doctrines of the faith so that they lost their biblical character was wrong.

The task of retooling theology for our generation is important, serious, and imperative, but dangerous. If we do not retool, we risk becoming obsolete and failing to reach our own generation. If we retool the wrong way, we retool the biblical faith out of existence. The great theological giants of the first part of the twentieth century had one great conviction in common: to restate the Christian faith so as to make it credible to men of the twentieth century. The worry of the evangelical is that men like Bultmann and Tillich retranslated the Christian faith out of existence. This is the danger of restating the Christian faith. In our zeal to be contemporary we may lose our biblical foundation and present a modernized unbiblical version of Christianity.

The modern evangelical wishes to restate his Christian faith in light of the latest knowledge of biblical archeology. He wishes to use the best lexical and exegetical tools to be found in our modern theological libraries. He wants to be informed of modern science, modern psychology, and modern philosophy so that even if he may not borrow from them he will not offend what is of essential truth in them.

In retranslating, restating, or retooling our Christian theology we will make mistakes. We may attempt to restate the doctrine of the Trinity or the incarnation and concede too much to the modern mind. Our new words may not be as accurate as the old ones as much as it is dinned into our ears that the old ones are obsolete. But if the risk of retranslating is to betray the faith, the failure to retranslate is to make the faith opaque to our generation. Either way we run a risk, and so the risk we must run. The Enlightenment has told us that modern man wishes to hear the gospel in modern concepts, modern models, and contemporary speech. The evangelical takes up this challenge, but as he does, he, perhaps more than any other kind of theologian, knows the risks involved in such a task. To be modern and yet biblical; to be biblical and yet contemporary; that's the rub.[6]

NOTES

1. For a general survey, see Paul Hazard, *The European Mind: 1680–1715* (Magnolia, Mass.: Peter Smith, 1963), and *European Thought in the Eighteenth Century* (Magnolia, Mass.: Peter Smith, 1963); J. H. Randall, Jr., *The Making of the Modern Mind*, rev. ed. (Boston: Houghton Mifflin, 1940); Peter Gay, *The Enlightenment: An Interpretation* (New York: Alfred A. Knopf, 1969), and *The Enlightenment: The Rise of Modern Paganism* (New York: Random House, 1968); Ernst Cassirer, *The Philosophy of the Enlightenment* (Boston: Beacon Press, 1955).

See also C. G. Shaw, "The Enlightenment," *Encyclopedia of Religion and Ethics*, ed. James Hastings (New York: Charles Scribner's Sons, 1908–27) 5:310–16; C. Brinton, "The Enlightenment," *Encyclopedia of Philosophy*, ed. P. Edwards (New York: Macmillan, 1967), 2:519–25.

Two books which show especially how the Enlightenment spilled over into Christianity are: Gilbert Highet, *The Classical Tradition* (New York: Oxford University Press, 1949), and A. Richardson, *History, Sacred and Profane* (Philadelphia: Westminster, 1964).

2. *Sacramentum Mundi: An Encyclopedia of Theology*, ed. Karl Rahner (New York: Herder and Herder, 1969), 2:230.

3. The Enlightenment brought in the back door much of the doctrine of sin that it threw out the front door. See Cassirer, *Philosophy of the Enlightenment*, pp. 137–60.

4. Ibid., p. 161.

5. Helmut Thielicke, *Between Heaven and Earth* (New York: Harper & Row, 1965), chap. 2, "Historical Criticism of the Bible: The historical-critical study of Scripture. A conversation with fundamentalism."

6. Perhaps no book in modern times shows the agony of this rub better than Hans Küng, *Infallible? An Inquiry* (Garden City: Doubleday, 1971). Küng is caught trying to be a faithful Roman Catholic theologian and at the same time trying to come to terms with all the materials historians have unearthed concerning historical shoddiness in many Roman Catholic doctrinal definitions.

Chapter Six

THE COLLISION OF LIBERALISM WITH EVANGELICAL THEOLOGY

Section 21: Schleiermacher

In his book *The Impact of American Religious Liberalism* Kenneth Cauthen makes a distinction between liberalism and modernism. Liberal theologians attempt to retain significance for Holy Scripture and Jesus Christ. Modernist theologians work principally with a philosophy of religion and may or may not say anything about Holy Scripture and Jesus. In this chapter, however, I will deal with the terms *liberal* and *modernist* as synonyms.

Peter Gay gives as a subtitle for his book on the Enlightenment, *The Rise of Modern Paganism*. The reason is that the majority of the intellectuals of Europe gave up orthodox Protestantism and turned to the positive, life-affirming attitude of the ancient Greeks and Romans.

But some scholars did not believe that the Enlightenment was fatal for Christianity. If Christianity were restated in light of the progress of the Enlightenment, then Christianity could still be believable. The first theologian to attempt such a reconstruction of Christian theology was Friedrich Schleiermacher (1768–1834). In 1799 he published his new platform for the reconstruction of Christianity in a book entitled *On Religion: Speeches to Its Cultured Despisers*.

This book was not addressed to the ordinary man but to the intellectual. Because of the Enlightenment intellectuals believed that Christianity was no longer believable so they—to use Schleiermacher's

word—despised (*verachten,* "despise, scorn, disdain") Christianity.
If these despisers really understood the essence of Christianity and
not its orthodox trappings, they could in intellectual integrity return
to the Christian faith. But how does Schleiermacher in detail expect
to make converts of these educated and cultured despisers?

Schleiermacher believes that their intelligence must not be insulted.
The Enlightenment cannot be repudiated or undone. Science is not
to be countered. Biblical criticism is not to be rejected. Biblicism cannot reject modern philosophy, nor can the demands of scientific history be ignored.

In Barth's essay on Schleiermacher in *Protestant Thought: From
Rousseau to Ritschl* (German title: *Protestant Theology in the Nineteenth Century*), he repeats over and over that Schleiermacher
wants to be a modern man. He does not wish to go behind modern
knowledge and modern progress. Therefore, Schleiermacher asks no
retreat to the past from his educated readers.

*The cultured German must be told that religion is not dogma,
creed, or confession but a living experience with God.* The historic
stance of both the Roman Catholic church and orthodox Protestantism is that truth in the form of theology determines, shapes,
and tests religious experience. This is now reversed. Faith as the subjective or internal disposition of man is made more fundamental than
faith as that which is to be believed. This is nothing short of a
Copernican revolution in theology. But only by this strategy can
Schleiermacher hope to recapture the German intellectuals.

In order to make this Copernican revolution, Schleiermacher had
to do some profound rethinking of what faith is. Schleiermacher was
heir to German idealist philosophy, and it is somewhat difficult to
grasp his idea without some background in philosophy, but nevertheless the attempt must be made. The essence of faith to Schleiermacher was feeling. But Schleiermacher did not mean feeling in the
ordinary sense of a sensation ("I have a feeling I am falling") or an
emotional tone ("I feel happy about my birthday present"). Feeling
(*Gefühl*) was a philosophical concept to him, not a psychological
one. The term *feeling* involved rapport or empathy with the universe.
Schleiermacher was a romantic, and he believed that there was a
unity and a communion among God, man, and nature. This unity or
communion was mediated by feeling.

But it was not just any feeling. It was feeling at its maximum.
Schleiermacher said that it was a feeling of absolute dependence upon

God. A feeling of respect and love for one's parents was not a religious feeling because it was not absolute. Faith then, as an attitude, is a feeling of absolute dependence upon God and not a rational assent to dogma.

Schleiermacher further did not appeal to the intellectuals with a positivistic biblicism. Positivistic biblicism comes out at the popular level in the expression, "I believe the Bible from cover to cover and also the covers." Schleiermacher did not come to them saying, "If it is in the Bible, I believe it."

Schleiermacher approached these intellectuals with a very articulate philosophy. The intellectuals were not asked to swallow the Bible. To the contrary, the particular philosophy of Schleiermacher laid the foundations of religion as a universal phenomenon in the universe and man as religious being. Religion was made a natural part of the universe and human experience like chairs, tables, stars, and sunrises. There is a universal Spirit which seeks communion with the human spirit, and this is the stuff religion is made of.

Religion is, according to this redefinition of it, a special kind of psychological state. It has already been said that it is a feeling of absolute dependence upon God. But these feelings as a fundamental way of perceiving and contacting Reality may also be stated as a kind of consciousness. When man has this feeling of absolute dependence upon God, he thereby has a God-consciousness. Sin is a lack of this God-consciousness. The problem is how this lack of God-consciousness can be corrected and man raised to God-consciousness. This act of going from a consciousness of sensuality or sensuousness to God-consciousness is redemption.

At this point Schleiermacher introduces the Christian dimension to his religion. It was Christ who had this perfect God-consciousness. It was so strong in him that even the torment, confusion, and death of the cross could not destroy it. Therefore as Christ is preached in the church, men are called away from their sinful sensuous consciousness to God-consciousness. In this transition they are then redeemed, and in that Christ is the catalyst of this transition he is our Redeemer. Here then is the gospel in new and modern philosophical garments that a modern intellectual can believe and not the older gospel of Lutheran orthodoxy that so offended the German intellectuals.

Schleiermacher also tells these intellectuals that the day of man's religious childhood is over and we no longer need believe in miracles.

A Christian does not have to believe iron axe-heads float, or that fire
falls from heaven and consumes wet wood, or that Jesus walked on
water, or that his crucified body rose from the dead. The scientific
understanding of the natural order is not challenged. Religion is
within the bounds of the natural order.

But there is yet another gain for Schleiermacher in rejecting the
supernatural: Religion shines as true in its own light. It needs no
artificial support from the outside like a miracle. It requires no cre-
dentials outside of itself like the resurrection of a corpse. Religion is
part of the fabric of the universe and is therefore as natural to man
as the air he breathes and the water he drinks. Omit the scandal of
the miraculous and nothing stands in the way of the intellectual's
return to the Christian faith.

*All of the dogmas of orthodox Lutheranism can be restated in a
modern acceptable way, and what cannot be restated can be discarded.* The title in German of Schleiermacher's major book in
theology is *Der christliche Glaube nach den Grundsätzen der evan-
gelischen Kirche in Zusammenhang dargestellt.* I have inserted the
German title because it does not appear in the English translation
of it by H. R. Makintosh and J. S. Steward who gave it the title, *The
Christian Faith.*

But the full German title is highly revelatory of Schleiermacher's
idea of Christian theology. The word *faith (Glaube)* is used rather
than dogma or dogmatics to indicate the subjective, personal, experiential character of doctrine in contrast to objectionable, ecclesiastically defined dogma which we have seen was despised by the
Enlightenment.

The essential doctrines (*Grundsätzen*) are to be stated in their
inner connection (*Zusammenhang*). Not all traditional dogma is to
be treated but only that which conforms to Schleiermacher's concept
of doctrine, hence he limits himself to fundamental assertions
(*Grundsätzen*). But again, these fundamental assertions must be
correlated with the one fundamental assertion, namely, redemption
through Christ as Schleiermacher has spelled out the nature of this
redemption. If a doctrine cannot be linked to this fundamental assertion, it is to be discarded.

The preexistence of Christ or the doctrine of angels plays no part
in the fundamental assertions of the Christian religion and may be
discarded. Here again much of the kind of theological materials the
cultured despisers could no longer bring themselves to believe is

discarded so they can be Christians without having to believe them.

With these matters in mind, it should then be fairly easy to comprehend Schleiermacher's fundamental definition of the Christian religion:

> Christianity is a monotheistic faith, belonging to the teleological [ethical] type of religion, and is essentially distinguished from other such faiths [Judaism, Islam] by the fact that in it everything has relation to the redemption accomplished by Jesus of Nazareth.[1]

Here then, in the most elementary way, are the ingredients of liberal Christianity. Not all liberal Christianity is a carbon copy of Schleiermacher, for there are different versions of liberal Christianity, but Schleiermacher was the pioneer in this kind of reconstruction of the Christian religion.

Section 22: American religious liberalism

To trace the course of religious liberalism through German and English theology would take us too far afield for our specific concern of the status of evangelical theology in America. I have sketched out the bare elements of Schleiermacher's system to show how one man attempted to salvage Christianity from the mortal wound of the Enlightenment and in so doing founded religious liberalism.

Schleiermacher exerted a profound influence on German theology, but he founded no school. The most influential religious liberal theologian after Schleiermacher was Albrecht Ritschl (1822–89). The great German theologians just before World War I, under whom the founders of neoorthodoxy studied, were disciples of Ritschl (Herrmann, Harnack). The basic species of liberalism that spread to England and America was Ritschlianism. Another version of liberalism stemmed from the philosophy of Hegel (for example, Biedermann), but its influence on American theology was indirect. There were other forces in America which helped create American religious liberalism besides German and English versions of Ritschlianism, for example Coleridge's *Aids to Reflection*.

The story of early American theology is the story of how the original Calvinistic theology of the Puritan settlers underwent successive changes until it ended with the new theology. Part of this story involves the emergence of Unitarianism whose outspoken leader was W. E. Channing. The theology of German and English liberalism was then absorbed into the new theology developing on American soil and together they formed American religious liberalism.

Three books specialize in tracing the course of liberalism in America: L. H. DeWolf, *The Case for Theology in Liberal Perspective*; H. P. Van Dusen, *The Vindication of Liberal Theology*; and K. Cauthen, *The Impact of American Religious Liberalism*. In that Cauthen's book is clearly outlined and states the principles of liberal theology with such clarity, I will use it as the basis of describing liberal theology in America.

Cauthen finds the essence of American liberalism in three concepts: *continuity, autonomy,* and *dynamism.* Each of these concepts represents a contradiction to Christianity as understood in the traditions of Protestant orthodoxy and evangelicalism. Religious liberalism came into existence as a strategy to preserve Christianity after the devastating attacks against Protestant orthodoxy in the Enlightenment. These three concepts are then to be seen as products of the Enlightenment.

Continuity. Christian orthodoxy—Eastern, Roman, Protestant, evangelical—stresses the supernatural element in the Christian faith. Through the doctrines of creation, the Holy Spirit, and the immanence of God there is continuity in orthodoxy as it envisions God's relationship to his creation and to man. But in that man is a sinner, there is a supernatural and, therefore, discontinuous action of God in revelation and redemption.

Liberalism seeks to eliminate all such discontinuities as they cause Christianity to clash with science and the kind of universe the sciences project. On the positive side, liberalism sees a continuity between God, man, and creation. In this continuity there is no clash or conflict with science. After a historical survey of the problem of continuity, Cauthen lists nine results of the application of continuity to liberal theology:[2]

(1) The historic division between nature and grace, the natural and the supernatural, is eliminated, and a new theory of the presence of God in his universe is expounded. The supernatural is no longer something perpendicular from heaven intersecting our time-world line, but the supernatural is a stratum within the natural order of the universe. The primary relationship of God to the universe is one of immanence, and the supernatural is a segment of this immanence, otherwise we would be pure positivists or naturalists or

materialists. This is not pantheism but panentheism. God is in all things without being all things.

(2) The supernatural in the form of miracles which had become a major element in the apologetics of orthodoxy is rejected.

Hume (1711–76) made the first serious attack on miracles as recorded in Scripture (although historically speaking it was really his reaction to Roman Catholic claims to miracles, which he experienced in his sojourn in France, which turned him away from miracles, and not the patient study of the New Testament itself). However, it was Schleiermacher within the Christian church who repudiated miracles. He advises: "We should abandon the idea of the *absolutely* supernatural because no single instance of it can be known by us, and we are nowhere required to believe it." [3] This accurately represents the liberal viewpoint toward miracles. In the preliminary remarks preceding the citation from Schleiermacher, he says that it is the mandate of science that Christians surrender the concept of the "absolutely supernatural."

(3) Revelation is not a breaking into our world from heaven with knowledge that a man as sinner could never attain. There is no special revelation or soteric revelation. Revelation is a dimension of knowing within our natural world expressed by such words as *insight, intuition,* or *discovery.*

(4) Man is stressed as being good even though he may be wayward. He certainly is not totally depraved. The entire liberal program in theology is a repudiation of sin as an offense to the holiness or justice of God to which God responds in wrath and judgment.

(5) There is a radical alteration of historic Christology. The historic orthodox doctrine of the incarnation of God the Son in Jesus of Nazareth, his conception by the Holy Spirit and birth from the Virgin Mary, his sacrificial death on the cross for the sins of the world, his bodily resurrection, and his ascension to heaven are all rejected or subjected to radical reinterpretation so that the original orthodox substance is gone.

Christ is now the God-filled man, or the perfect man before God, or the archetypal man (*Urbild*) of all spiritual or religious men. He is unique only in the sense that God adopted him to reveal in the spiritual quality of his life perfect manhood before God. He thereby reveals our sins in revealing our shortcomings, and he is our Redeemer in that he calls us to the real spiritual life (phrased differently by each liberal theologian).

Some liberals startled the theological world by calling Jesus the first Christian. In essence they were saying that Christianity is the religion that Jesus practiced, the religious or spiritual ideal of all men and not the religion about Jesus. This idea was in contrast to orthodoxy which admonished "believe on the Lord Jesus Christ and thou shalt be saved." Historically the Christian church has put primacy in faith as that which is believed, expressed in the commonly accepted Latin formula: *fides quae creditur.* Faith as the personal and subjective response in religion is designated in an equally traditional Latin formula: *fides qua creditur.* Schleiermacher reversed the historic order of these two phrases, and all liberalism went with him. If Jesus Christ is my Lord and Redeemer in the traditional sense, then I believe in the religion about Jesus. Jesus is not a Christian but the Redeemer of Christians. But if Jesus is the archetypal spiritual man (*Urbild*), the adopted son of God, the one who practiced true piety, then Jesus is the first Christian. Christians are the images struck off from the original—expressed in the German by *Abbild* (*Ur-* means primitive, primeval, original; *Bild* means a picture; *Ab-* means away from, off; thus the original is the *Urbild* and the copy is the *Abbild*).

(6) Especially in America the slogan, "The Fatherhood of God and the brotherhood of man," became the most fundamental assertion of liberal theology. On the one hand, it is an affirmation of universalism. The categories of *saved* and *lost* are scrapped in that all men are brothers and therefore God's children, which is also true if God is every man's Father. It also implied the Social Gospel. All men, individual and corporate, privately and socially, were to be treated with the ethic of love.

(7) Traditional eschatology is rejected. There is neither heaven nor hell in the traditional sense. Eternal life is a quality of spiritual life that begins here in this life. The eschatology of liberalism revolved around two concepts. Historically liberalism believed in the gradual extension of the kingdom of God until—it was hoped—it would Christianize all of man's institutions. Liberalism was also very strong in teaching personal immortality but rejecting the resurrection of the body as a "gross material concept."

(8) The concept of Christian and non-Christian, saved and lost, believer and unbeliever, became relativized. If a person consciously tried to follow the Christian way of life in worship and morality, he was a Christian in name; people who did not follow such a way of

life were non-Christians. But the absolute division of saved and lost with two separate destinies in the world to come was rejected.

(9) The concepts of church and world were relativized. The church is really open to the world. The church and the kingdom of God are planted together within the world in an almost literal sense. The church is to Christianize the world which means to induce all human institutes to function according to the Christian ethic.

Autonomy. The Enlightenment taught that man was on his own. His reason was adequate for the solution of all his problems. Dependence upon the supernatural in any manner or form was not necessary. Religious liberalism was heir to the autonomy of the Enlightenment. Man did not need revelation for knowledge, or an incarnation for redemption, or miracles for assurance.

In rejecting Holy Scripture as the revealed, inspired, infallible, and authoritative Word of God and relocating its normative character in the religious experiences it suggests, and in turning man to his own reason and experience as further courts of appeal, certain theological conclusions follow:

(1) The ultimate foundation of religion is man's religious experiences, and Scripture is normative only within this context.

(2) Schleiermacher's reversal of faith from the doctrine believed as secondary to faith as the experience of religion takes over with a vengeance. In orthodox Protestantism, theology was prior to experience, shaped it, and criticized it. In liberalism, experience becomes the fundamental stratum of religion and theology is secondary as the act of reflecting upon experience.

Liberal theologians believed that man as a rational creature must bring reason into religion as he brings it into all things. Furthermore, without some sort of reference to reason there are no adequate checks against fanaticism. But on the other hand, the concept of a binding creed and a normative theology are no longer possible in the church. All theology that is written is transitional and provisional, and it is always fair play to attempt a total rewrite of theology.

(3) Revelation as a supernatural communication to man of the truths about God, creation, and man gives way to the autonomy of reason; to the self-validating power of religious experiences; to revelation as really insight or intuition or discovery.[4]

(4) Only those theological statements may be admitted into theology that are capable of an experiential response. This was started by Schleiermacher (feeling) and continued by Ritschl (value).

For example, I can have no real spiritual response to the preexistence
of Christ as I can have to the love of God. Therefore, the preexistence of Christ is not a proper topic of theology. Or, I can have no
response to the Trinity as stated in the Athanasian Creed, but I can
respond to the Holy Spirit present in all human relationships.

(5) With the rejection of Scripture as the Word of God revealed,
and revelation not seen as God's self-disclosure of truth, then dogma
becomes no longer central to the life of the church or crucial to its
existence. Religion is essentially psychological or experiential or
ethical or concerned with social reconstruction. The new Apostles'
Creed is "Dogma divides; service unites." The typical debate over
dogmatic issues which was characteristic of the church in the patristic
and Reformation periods is now passé.

Dynamism. The concepts of history and of the universe as developed in the nineteenth century were in terms of movement, change,
progress, and development. The universe is not a fixed, static system
of laws. As a result, everything was seen in change or transit or
evolution. Fixed dogmas or unchanging fundamentals of religion
were out of harmony with the nature of both science and the universe.

(1) Theological systems are tentative postulations and should
never attempt to be once-for-fall formulations.

(2) The Social Gospel means that the Christian ethic of love
is a progressive, moving, changing force that would permeate all of
society and by permeating it transform it.

(3) The theory of evolution meant a total reinterpretation of the
doctrine of creation, the origin of man, the Fall, and original sin.
According to liberalism man fell upward. This paradoxical expression means that when man felt guilty it meant he had a conscience
so that the very feeling of guilt meant another upward evolutionary
step had been taken.

(4) The doctrine of the divine immanence developed in the
preceding discussion is reenforced by the progress of science. Science
seen in categories of progress, process, and development coincides
with the immanental manner in which God is related to his creation.

(5) The study of comparative religions led scholars to see Christianity as the best religion or the religion for the cultural West but
not the unique or final or absolute religion. All religions are different
ways of expressing certain common elements which they share with
each other. Alan W. Watts's *The Meaning of Happiness: The Quest
for Freedom of the Spirit in Modern Psychology and the Wisdom of*

the East is typical of this newer mentality in aproaching the religions of the world.

(6) Revelation is also reinterpreted in view of dynamism. Revelation is not a finished body of truth sealed in Scripture but is an ongoing process striving for better and better moral insights and higher values.

(7) Dynamism reshapes eschatology. Man is progressing morally in this life and in the world to come.[5] Traditional eschatological topics like the second coming of Christ, the millennial reign, or the bodily resurrection of believers are no longer believable.

(8) If all the universe in its every dimension is in process, and all is the product of process, then Christianity is a natural product of history, the New Testament documents are the natural products of sociological and religious forces, and the Christian church is a natural product of the situation within the Roman Empire in the first Christian century. This can be verified by intensive researches into pre-Christian history, the Christian history of the first century, and the developments within the second Christian century.

In summary, religious liberalism believed that the forms and expressions that the early church took were wrong, but their intention or spirit was right. Jesus Christ was a remarkable person, but he was not God incarnate; and Holy Scripture was a wonderful religious book, but it was not infallibly inspired by the Holy Spirit. So the religious liberals felt that they were in continuity with real Christianity even though they might have violent disagreements with the orthodox and the fundamentalists. In fact, they readily claimed that they had the best version of Christianity, for it was one that modern man could believe without the sacrifice of his scholarship, science, or intellect.

Section 23: The evangelical response to religious liberalism

Evangelicals under many different flags eventually recognized that the new liberal theology was not another version of historic Christianity but a contradiction to it. The evangelical response was diverse.

Those in Germany who still carried on the Pietistic tradition were not slow in realizing that historic orthodoxy and liberalism were two divergent theologies. From the inception of modernism until the days of Bultmann and Tillich, they have fought theological innovations.

In the theological world some sort of synthesis or compromise was attempted. Schleiermacher's vitalistic concept of faith and his Christocentric theology were appealing, but his radical denials could not be accepted. One such compromise was known as mediating theology (*Vermittlungstheologie*). Other scolars did not resist modern biblical criticism but said that it did not interfere with the serious task of biblical exegesis. These men were known as biblical realists. The Erlangen school under the leadership of von Hofmann attempted to make a synthesis of Schleiermacher's insights with a special view of biblical history (*Heilsgeschichte*, "holy history"). The biblicists (*Biblizismus*) simply turned their backs on biblical criticism and liberal theology.

The reaction in America was confused. Many ministers who could not distinguish the theological nuances of the debate thought liberals and evangelicals were saying the same thing only in different words. The conflict was apparent, not real. Others thought that theological pluralism had always been in the church and this was but another phase of it. The motto should be "live and let live."

The astute and learned evangelical theologian was convinced that liberal theology and evangelical theology were not friendly alternatives but diametrically opposed to each other. Machen, one of the most learned on the evangelical side, insisted in his book, *Christianity and Liberalism*, that Christianity as historically understood and Christianity as reinterpreted by liberalism were two different religions.[6]

The evangelical response to liberalism operated on two levels: (1) The fundamentalist minister or evangelist or Bible teacher attacked liberalism loudly from the pulpit and strongly in print as a deviation of the faith once for all delivered to the saints (Jude 3). (2) Learned theologians, like Kuyper, Lecerf, Orr, Warfield, and Machen, using accepted scholarly methods and standards attempted to show how the fundamental assumptions and particular doctrines of liberalism were at variance with the fundamental assumptions and particular doctrines of historic Christianity.

In a sense the most important successful counteraction of the fundamentalists to the modernist invasion was to institutionalize fundamentalism. They felt that institutions would give fundamentalism permanence as well as places of entrenchment and defense.

The Bible conference. The Bible conference took many shapes. Its most permanent shape was an actual camp with buildings and an established program. From weekly meetings to expanded summer programs, many eventually became around-the-year operations. Today there is a vast network of such conference grounds, large and small, from ocean to ocean and border to border. Many of them have formed a league, so to speak, called the Christian Camping Association.

These more durable conferences have been supplemented by many others such as weekly conferences in some central church in a large city, or a special congress, or a conference conducted by some Christian school.

Evangelism. The fundamentalists took the Great Commission with great seriousness. This meant a persistent evangelistic activity. Out of this effort emerged great name evangelists as Moody, Alexander, Torrey, and Sunday. Besides such name evangelists there were scores of relatively unknowns who were professional evangelists. Their entire ministry was that of going from city to city, hall to hall, or church to church holding evangelistic meetings.

There was another dimension to this evangelism, and that was the fundamentalists' conviction that each Christian must be an evangelist—a personal worker or a soul winner. Moody was taken as the model, for he pledged God he would never go to bed at night until he had witnessed to at least one person that day. Many classes were set up on personal work and soul winning. Numerous booklets were published on how personal work should be done.

Bible institutes. Although the first Bible institutes were the *Collegia Philobiblica* of the Pietists, it was D. L. Moody and his followers who made the Bible institute the educational stronghold of fundamentalism. Beginning with the Moody Bible Institute and then the Bible Institute of Los Angeles, Bible institutes spread throughout America so that there is one in every large city and several in the very large cities. Some of these have moved on to become Bible colleges, and some have even become liberal arts colleges. But they form the one continuum of the institutionalizing of the fundamentalist movement. Some of the smaller, more Pentecostal churches have chosen the Bible institute over the college or seminary as the kind of school they desire for the training of their ministers.

Publishing. D. L. Moody not only saw the importance of the Bible conference, the evangelistic crusade, and the Bible institute, but he realized the importance of the printed page. So he institutionalized fundamentalistic publishing, one of the biggest operations of fundamentalism. Fundamentalist presses have printed tracts by the hundreds of millions, as well as pamphlets, booklets, magazines, and books. A number of independent fundamentalist publishing houses exist today which turn out an unbelievable tonnage of material from Sunday school lessons to some high-level academic books.

The most famous of all the fundamentalist publications was *The Fundamentals*. These were a series of booklets eventually bound into four volumes underwritten by the Stewart brothers of Los Angeles. The authors ranged from important pastors and successful evangelists to learned evangelical professors in important theological seminaries. These booklets—more than a million copies—were distributed free of charge to all who requested them. Although much literature on fundamentalism takes *The Fundamentals* as definitive literature, this is not quite the case. The history of the fundamentalist movement was not simply an extension of *The Fundamentals*. Some of the authors who wrote essays in the *The Fundamentals* would not be welcome in the strict fundamentalistic circles that developed later in the thirties and following decades.

The fundamentalists also turned out a glut of journals or magazines. Most of these were short-lived, but some received an enormous circulation, or a very influential circulation. Even in the present decade the avalanche of fundamentalist literature is so great that no person could hope to read all of it that is published in any given month.

Fellowships. Efforts to consolidate and unify fundamentalists were made by forming various fundamentalist groups such as the World's Christian Fundamentals Association. In some cities a premillennial fellowship was formed as a functionally antimodernist association. Today the National Association of Evangelicals attempts to bind evangelicals together as persons and as denominations. An International Council of Christian Churches has been formed to counteract the World Council of Churches. It must be said that the impact or influence of such groups, especially the various older national and world fundamentalist organizations, has been very uneven and the results disappointing.

Radio. One of the most successful of all fundamentalist efforts to institutionalize was through the radio. This was done either by owning and operating one's own radio station as some churches and schools did, or by buying time on local stations and national networks. Charles Fuller, Percy Crawford, Walter Maier, and Oral

Roberts were among the more successful radio speakers. The most influential of them all with the largest coverage was the "Old Fashioned Revival Hour." Many of these programs were one hour long, a phenomenon that was perhaps never to be witnessed again due to the manner in which television has changed radio broadcasting.

It must be mentioned that part of the amazing phenomenon of fundamentalist radio was that the fundamentalists bought their own time while the denominational or interdenominational groups were given free time by the networks. One doubts if Harry Emerson Fosdick could have supported his weekly Sunday broadcast heard coast to coast by contributions from his liberal Christian audience.

Specialized evangelism. Fundamentalists felt that certain groups needed a specialized kind of evangelism, and so specialized evangelistic organizations grew up. A number of groups specialized in Jewish evangelism, others in rural evangelism, and still others in Mormon evangelism.

Faith missions. In order to bypass the policies of denominations who sent out missionaries of liberal theological convictions as well as evangelicals (the "inclusive policy"), many independent or faith missionary societies came into existence. In this the fundamentalists were preeminently successful if one judges solely by statistics. It is estimated that at the peak of their success these faith missions or independent missionary societies provided approximately 75 percent of the missionary personnel of the world. The amount of money diverted from customary denominational giving was certainly an enormous sum.

The Scofield Reference Bible. Although not all users of the Scofield Reference Bible were fundamentalists, it did become the Bible of the fundamentalists. As time progressed fundamentalism defended not only fundamentals of the faith but dispensational and premillennial theology. This theology was beautifully and systematically expressed in the Scofield Reference Bible.

Although scorned by academic biblical and theological scholars, this Bible nevertheless had certain special advantages.

First, the doctrinal footnotes are in the historic Protestant tradition and written with such finesse and skill that they have been able to satisfy readers from an unbelievable number of divergent theological traditions. Writing notes with such a wide interdenominational acceptance was a rare achievement. Second, the literary style of the

English is masterful. Whether it was Scofield's training in English or training in law (for Scofield was a lawyer), the result was a lucidity and compactness of exposition. Third, it gave the layman a way of putting his entire Bible together. Topical sermons and desultory Bible studies do not give the Christian a sense of the unity of Scripture, or of the progress of revelation in Scripture, or of how parts of Scripture fit together. No other reference Bible was or has been able to compete with it on this score. As much as the technical scholar may object to the dispensationalism that schematizes biblical history, he cannot deny the fact that for thousands of laymen the Scofield Reference Bible did unify the Bible.

There was another interesting facet to the dispensational and premillennial views of so many fundamentalists and as set forth in the Scofield Reference Bible. The fundamentalists considered dispensationalism and premillennialism enduring bulwarks against liberalism. They would ask: Who ever heard of a dispensational, premillennial liberal? Of course, there are no dispensational, premillennial liberals! The conclusion was then drawn that if a believer, or a school, or a denomination stayed very close to a dispensational and premillennial theology it would have the strongest possible defense against any inroads of liberalism or dilution of orthodox theology or defection to liberal theology.

Certain practices of the liberals greatly aggravated the fundamentalists.

The fundamentalists deeply resented the manner in which great historic doctrines were not only discarded but mocked, ridiculed, and derided. Fundamentalists felt a double hypocrisy in this activity of the liberals. First, the liberals claimed to be Christians and yet were denying those essentials which for many centuries had been part of the very definition of what it meant to be a Christian. Secondly, as apostles of love the liberals were hardly exhibiting love when they so ruthlessly ridiculed the doctrines of the fundamentalists and yet would be so gracious toward adherents of non-Christian religions.

The fundamentalists further felt an element of deliberate dishonesty in the claim of the liberals that they really did believe the historic doctrines only in a different framework. Certainly they believed in the deity of Christ—meaning that Christ was the most God-filled man who ever lived. They believed in the Trinity—meaning that God's action in the world was complex. They believed in original sin—meaning the corporate character of sin as seen in the sinful structures of society. They firmly believed the Bible to be the Word of God—meaning that the normative religious experiences for Christians were to be found in the experiences of the great religious personalities of the Bible. They were true disciples of the Reformers—meaning that as the Reformers stood for religious liberty against the Roman Catholic church so they too stood for religious liberty.

The fundamentalists thought the liberals inconsistent in that they would subject the Scriptures to higher criticism but would not in turn subject their higher criticism to a higher critical critique of its assumptions. The true impartiality of a scholar would be that he would be as willing to subject his own procedures to critical review as he subjected the Scriptures to critical scrutiny.

The fundamentalists seriously objected to the extension of biological evolution to religion as a model for the reconstruction of religion, and particularly of biblical religion. The liberal reasoned that if all is in the state of change or process or evolution so must have been the religion of Israel and the theology of the New Testament church. They therefore applied an evolutionary schema to reconstruct both of them and by so doing eliminated the special acts of God in revelation and redemption.

However, a major problem has to be confronted: What is a fundamental doctrine?

The idea of a list of central doctrines of the Christian faith is not something new with fundamentalists. The Apostles' Creed was supposed to contain the essence of the Christian faith. Many theologians consider the Nicene Creed (of A.D. 381) the finest summary of the Christian religion. The Roman Catholic church has its *de fide* ("of the faith") teachings which all Roman Catholics must believe. There are doctrines considered so important that the church stands or falls with them (*articulus stantis et cadentis Ecclesiae*).

To the fundamentalist a fundamental doctrine is one of such importance to the Christian faith that if denied the faith itself would collapse. Some doctrines may be very important such as the doctrine of baptism. But Christians may vary in their understanding of baptism, and Christianity and the church still stand. Differences between a Presbyterian and an Anglican are not fatal. But the difference between a fundamentalist and a liberal is fatal according to the fundamentalists. The liberal is not offering variant views that have been honored as viable options in the history of theology; the liberal is cutting out the very core of Christianity itself. If the liberal denials are true, then Christianity as known for almost two thousand years has ceased to exist. The fundamentals are therefore that cluster of doctrines that are nonnegotiable; they have no viable alternatives. Destroy this theological cluster and you destroy Christianity.

The problem with such a cluster is that it is easier said than done. Who determines what belongs in the cluster? Unfortunately some of the doctrines were more directed toward the denials of the liberals than toward establishing what is absolutely indispensable to Christian faith. Any list of fundamental doctrines is a human venture and liable to human error. In principle the fundamentalists could well have been right, but the various lists of fundamentals (for several have been made) are open to evaluation and criticism.

In many studies of fundamentalism by nonfundamentalists there is an element of distortion. The fundamentalist-modernist controversy was not comprised only of leading fundamentalist pulpiteers denouncing liberal professors. Into this battle came evangelical theologians of genuine academic stature, and they waged their battle in another way and at another level. It is this element of the controversy that seldom receives just treatment in works on the history of fundamentalism. There were a number of competent evangelical theologians who saw through the issues much better than the pulpiteering fundamentalist preacher, and their analysis of the issues needs to be heeded.

The first of these is Abraham Kuyper. Kuyper was raised in a typical Dutch orthodox Calvinistic home. When he went to the university, he shifted away from the orthodoxy of his home to the prevailing liberalism of his times. When the professor of theology at the university denounced the resurrection of Christ as unbelievable by a modern man, Kuyper joined in the cheering with the other students.

Upon completion of his university training he took a pastorate. His congregation was a mixture of the newer liberal Dutch churchman and the older orthodox Dutch Christian. When Kuyper called on the liberal members of his flock, he found them theologically confused, ambiguous and uncertain about their faith. When he called on the orthodox members, he found people who knew what they believed and why they believed it, and furthermore they believed it with a zest. This set Kuyper to musing. Why were the enlightened liberals so vague and so flat about their beliefs whereas the orthodox showed a conviction, a verve, and a certainty? The result was that Kuyper decided the orthodox members of his congregation had real Christianity. His reaction was that he forsook the liberal theology of his university days and returned to the orthodoxy of his home.

From that decision onward he became a transformed person. He became a theologian. He took five years really to learn Calvin. He became a journalist, an educator, and a politician.[7] During his lifetime he produced such a monumental literature that it took three volumes to record it all. His greatest works were *Theological Encyclopedia* in three volumes, the heart of which has been translated into English as *Principles of Sacred Theology* and *The Work of the Holy Spirit*. The latter was a series of popular articles written weekly for a religious journal but when bound together, in spite of their popular tone, turned out to be a most substantial theological work on the Holy Spirit, in fact, one of the best of the literature.

In reading Kuyper there is no question of his theological ability. He has been called the greatest Calvinist since Calvin. In interacting with liberalism he is more interested in Schleiermacher than Ritschl since he sees Schleiermacher as really the one who broke away from historic orthodoxy. He, perhaps, was also too close to Ritschl to see how his theology would eventually spread so much further and be so much more influential than that of Schleiermacher even though he lived late into the twentieth century. At any rate, he agrees with Barth that Schleiermacher is a greater theologian than Ritschl.

Kuyper praises Schleiermacher for restoring theology to the dignity of a science, and this is why Barth also admires Schleiermacher. This shows the academic competence of Kuyper. Kuyper does not flail and wail at Schleiermacher like a typical fundamentalist, for Kuyper is no theological novice. He knows where Schleiermacher has gone astray and hits him in his theological solar plexus. When Schleiermacher substituted feeling (in his profound theological understanding of the term), he had substituted a new fundamental for Christian theology. It is no longer the searching God for man but the exercise of a certain capacity within man to contact God and commune with him. But in so doing Schleiermacher lost the object of theology and therefore theology itself. In theology it is God who through special, divine, soteric (saving) revelation seeks man, and as such God is the object of theology making it a science. As great as

Schleiermacher's genius was, and as great as his effort was to reclaim Christianity's cultured and educated despisers, he failed in his attempt. He ends up with a theology with no object. This is a substantial criticism of liberalism with which an evangelical can concur for it represents a real critique and not the amateurish flailing of a fundamentalist.

Turning to James Orr's *The Christian View of God and the World,* we find a book as equally at home in German literature as English. Orr wrote a theological library of his own, but I will limit my remarks to this work. The liberals may well have criticized the ineptness of the fundamentalists' criticisms of liberalism, but that cannot be said of James Orr. No doubt fundamentalists had said some very ugly things about liberalism in the heat of the battle.[8]

When Orr deals with Schleiermacher, he does so with ease and competence. He concurs with Kuyper that even though Schleiermacher made a monumental effort to rehabilitate the dignity of Christian theology he surrendered that very objectivity which made theology a science. If feeling (*Gefühl*), not as mere emotion but the manner in which Romantic philosophers believed man contacted Reality of God, is the ultimate nature of religion and of the Christian experience, then Orr thinks that Schleiermacher has painted himself into a corner of religious subjectivity from which he cannot escape.[9] Perhaps Hegel's jibe, as trivial as it may seem, is the ultimate refutation of Schleiermacher. Hegel said that if absolute dependence was the mark of piety then the most pious creature he knew was his dog because he was certainly absolutely dependent upon Hegel for his existence.

When it came to the incarnation and the person of Christ, Schleiermacher seemed to say some remarkable things about Jesus. But when the exposition is looked at narrowly, Schleiermacher is saying that Jesus differs from us in degree but not in kind.[10] Thus the historic doctrine of the incarnation is scuttled. The same holds true of the cross. After the eloquent verbiage is sifted out, there is no vicarious death or vicarious atonement or bearing of sin, all of which are eloquently witnessed to in the pages of the New Testament.[11] In the historic sense of the word *atonement,* there is no atonement in Schleiermacher.[12]

Although Orr does not make the point in so many words, he has accurately indicated that Schleiermacher broke faith with historic Christianity. His views are not those of the Fathers or the Scholastics or the Reformers or the Protestant orthodox. It may be a religion, and it may even bear the name of Christianity, and it may vigorously wish to be identified with the Christian church, but it is not authentic Christianity.

The second great name in liberal theology is that of Ritschl, and for some years modernism was known by the term *Ritschlianism.* Orr devoted two books to Ritschl: *The Ritschlian Theology and Evangelical Faith* and *The Ritschlian Theology.*

Orr's criticism of Ritschl is quite detailed, and therefore we must limit ourselves to listing the principle points at which he criticizes Ritschl:

(1) Kant divided the world into the world of fact (*Critique of Pure Reason*) and of morality or religion (*Critique of Practical Reason*). Ritschl came under the philosophical spell of Kant but modified his Kantianism through the philosopher Lotze. In place of morality Lotze put value. According to Ritschl Scripture contains statements of fact and statements of value. The value statements are the religious or theological statements. That Jesus died on the cross is a factual statement; that I believe he died for me is a value statement. That Jesus was born of Mary is a factual statement; that he is the Son of God is a value statement. Orr believed that this division into factual statements and value statements could not be maintained. Furthermore, as much as Ritschl intended value statements also to be reality statements, unbelieving scientists and philosophers would consider Ritschl's value statements to be his purely subjective convictions.

(2) Ritschl's Christology is defective. If theological statements are value statements, then "Jesus is God" is a value statement and not a metaphysical or ontological statement. Orr thinks that there is an immense difference between "Jesus is God to me" as a functional or value statement, and the belief of the historic church in the deity of Christ.

(3) Ritschl's doctrine of sin is defective. Guilt to Ritschl was guilt feelings. Justification by faith was removing the guilty feelings from the consciousness of the sinner. According to Orr, Scripture teaches that sinners are really guilty before God and justification is the removal of guilt not merely of guilt feelings.

(4) Ritschl's doctrine of the atonement is faulty. It has been called the "moral influence theory." The purpose of the death of Christ is to demonstrate to man that God loves him regardless of his sin and

feelings of guilt and if man will but trust the revelation of God's love in the cross he will feel freed from his feelings of guilt and feel accepted as one of God's children. But such a view of the atonement cannot make peace with those verses that describe the cross as more than a revelation of love but also as some sort of objective transaction, or sacrifice, or act of atonement or reconciliation that is necessary because of man's sin.

(5) Ritschl's doctrine of revelation is a fiction. If God has truly spoken, then there is the objective fact of the Word of God, and Ritschl's distinction between judgments of fact and judgments of value is destroyed. If revelation is only in the realm of value judgments, it does not really say anything and therefore does not deserve to be called revelation.

Of course, there are other interpretations of Ritschl that grant him more fidelity to historic Christianity than Orr (for example, A. E. Garvie, *The Ritschlian Theology* and David Mueller, *An Introduction to the Theology of Albrecht Ritschl*). However, my point is that Orr is a responsible, competent theologian. He has endeavored to show that Schleiermacher and Ritschl in reinterpreting the Christian faith for the post-Enlightenment man reinterpreted it away. Not all the criticism of liberalism came from tirading fundamentalists. Much of it came from men of academic responsibility. Although Garvie and Mueller do not grant validity to all of Orr's criticisms, it would be unwise to take the opinions of such a learned man as Orr too lightly.

One American scholar who entered the combat on the side of evangelical theology was B. B. Warfield of Princeton Theological Seminary. Partly due to his invalid wife, and partly due to his own intense scholarly concerns, his daily life from year to year was a very narrow one. It was composed of going to the lecture room, to the library, and back home to help care for his wife. Consequently he never held a denominational post and made very few public appearances.

His controlling passion was to present Reformed theology as the truest and best version of Christian theology and to support that contention with the best possible scholarship and erudition of which he was capable. His major literary contributions were books, reviews of books in journals, articles in journals, and articles in religious encyclopedias.

Warfield's high level of scholarship is witnessed to by the fact that in contemporary continental studies on Augustine or Calvin, Warfield is uniformly acknowledged as the English language authority. This fact gains in significance when one realizes that Warfield died in 1921 and most books written at that time have long ago been replaced by further, more comprehensive studies.

Warfield does not dissect liberal theology in any one single volume, but discusses it here and there in his writings and book reviews. For example, in his small book, *The Plan of Salvation,* he discusses self-salvation (autosoterism—more familiarly, salvation by good works). He says liberalism is more heretical than Pelagius. Pelagius (the British monk who so vigorously opposed Augustine's theology in the patristic period) at least taught that man had to work out his salvation. Liberalism believes that all men are God's children, and therefore liberalism teaches universalism. In liberal theology man does nothing for his salvation because he is not really lost.

Harnack and Bousset (and many theologians influenced by them) had said that the Christian faith and the Christian gospel are summed up in the parable of the prodigal son. In showing that it was impossible to sum up the Christian gospel in this manner, Warfield wrote:

> Precious as this parable is for its great message that there is joy in heaven over one sinner that repents, when it is perverted from the purpose for which it was spoken and made to stand for the whole gospel . . . it becomes an instrument for tearing down *the entire fabric of Christianity.* There is no atonement in this parable, and indeed no Christ in even the most attenuated function which could possibly be ascribed to Christ. There is no creative grace in this parable; and indeed no Holy Spirit in any operation the most ineffective that could be attributed to him.[13]

One of the central beliefs of religious liberalism was that there is nothing supernatural in Christianity. Warfield wrote an article on Christian supernaturalism in which he stated that "the supernatural is the very breath of Christianity's nostrils and an anti-supernaturalistic atmosphere is to it the deadliest miasma. An absolutely anti-supernaturalistic Christianity is therefore a contradiction in terms."[14] The naturalistic versions of Christianity of Schleiermacher and Ritschl are not better versions but are actually self-destructive versions of historic Christianity.

Liberals carry over their antisupernatural bias into biblical criticism. Warfield believes that to write books refuting the liberal criticisms of Scripture is useless as long as liberals persist in being governed by their antisupernaturalism. The result is that "[liberal] theory follows theory with bewildering rapidity and—shall we not say it?—with equal bewildering levity while the [antisupernatural] conclusion remains the same." [15]

Warfield must be considered one of the greatest book reviewers of theological literature the Christian church has ever had. A Southern gentleman of the highest order, he always wrote with grace and polish. However, as one progresses through the review, he realizes that a first-class mind is at work, and soon through the gracefulness of spirit and politeness of vocabulary comes a devastating criticism. So remarkable were these reviews that the Oxford Press produced one whole volume of them—*Critical Reviews*. It is in these reviews that some of the most devastating criticisms of liberal theology made from the evangelical side are to be found.

Warfield's criticism of liberalism is that it is essentially a counterfeiting process. Liberal theologians use traditional theological concepts but invest them with such different meanings that they cease to be valid versions of the older meanings. The result of this process is that an entirely different religion is set forth from that which is understood as historic Christianity. Warfield's associate, Machen, made the most of this argument, but the original stems from Warfield. Such a master of historical theology as Warfield could not be fooled by words or by counterfeiting. He spotted the change in substance and assessed that the change in substance was so great that historic Christianity was lost.

Machen, also of Princeton Theological Seminary, led the fight in the Presbyterian church for evangelical theology. His unique personality, however, made him a matter of controversy. To many of his opponents he was hardly more than a sophisticated fundamentalist with such a controversial bent of mind that meaningful conversation with him was impossible. To those on his side he was a great warrior taking on the entire Presbyterian church almost single-handedly. The truth is somewhere between these extremes. Certainly as a student in Germany he was a *bon vivant*. Ned Stonehouse (*J. Gresham Machen: A Biographical Memoir*) records the happy association of the students with Machen. From time to time Machen would take his students out to dinner and for an evening of joviality. No doubt with the advancing years and the deepening of the controversy in the Presbyterian church, Machen might have lost some of his joviality and in the seriousness of conflict might have appeared cantankerous to those who opposed him.

First, let none doubt the academic ability of this man. His work in Germany was summed up in *The Origin of Paul's Religion* which is still considered one of the best summaries of Pauline studies of that period. *The Virgin Birth of Christ* is not a popular fundamentalist rant for the virgin birth but a careful historical and exegetical examination of the Matthew and Lucan accounts. More American preachers have learned their Greek from Machen's *New Testament Greek for Beginners* than any other grammar of the Greek New Testament. As of 1954 it was in its twenty-fourth edition and in 1972 is still listed in *Books in Print*. We cannot repeat here the whole story of Machen's academic career, but we are fortunate for Stonehouse's account of it.

When Machen became enmeshed in the Presbyterian conflict, he turned away from the academic book to the book that would communicate with the lay Presbyterian. Perhaps the most important of these works is *Christianity and Liberalism*. The thesis is not obscure. Liberalism is not another valid version of Christianity. It is a totally different religion than that taught in the New Testament. Presbyterians were asked to choose between Christianity as historically understood, especially in the Reformed confessions, and a new religion posing under the name of Christianity, using its vocabulary, and occupying its ecclesiastical offices. It was not difficult for an expert New Testament scholar like Machen to show that the theology of modernism or liberalism was not what the New Testament taught.

When asked if he were a fundamentalist, Machen's reply was that if one meant by a fundamentalist that certain doctrines could not be changed without destroying historic Christianity he was one with the fundamentalists. On the other hand he took strong exception to the term. Fundamental*ism* suggested something new or heretical, and that he did not believe. He stood for no modern *ism* but for the historic faith of the Christian church. Furthermore, he was a Reformed theologian. The richness of this heritage could not be reduced to five or six fundamentals but required an entire systematic theology to set the whole counsel of God before the church. Any nonevangelical who writes Machen off as only a sophisticated fundamentalist has not done him justice.[16]

Auguste Lecerf is virtually unknown to American fundamentalism.

He was, however, a rare genius and was called the last of the great French Calvinists. His *Introduction to Reformed Dogmatics* is a learned, historical, and creative work. Lecerf knows his philosophy, his cultural history, and his history of theology. Many of the earlier chapters of this book are not relevant today, but the later chapters contain rich booty for rethinking evangelical theology within the evangelical tradition.

Lecerf also knows his liberal theology, and he is one with Orr, Warfield, Kuyper, and Machen in affirming that liberalism is not Christianity. In putting experience prior to theology, and making faith a subjective attitude prior to faith as a dogmatic delivery, liberalism destroyed the dignity and objectivity of Christian theology. Again it may use traditional terms and refer to historic theologians, but it is not authentic Christianity. It is a strange product of the Enlightenment in which the endeavor to save Christianity only managed to eliminate it.

To sum up, the charge of liberals that fundamentalism is not really respectable theological scholarship may be true, but it is not the whole story. The whole story is that there were theologians just as educated, just as learned, and just as intellectually competent as the liberals who rejected liberalism as authentic Christianity. They backed up their charges with their mastery of biblical materials, their knowledge of historical theology, and their own thorough comprehension of Reformed theology. One may disagree with their judgments, but one cannot write them off as uninformed fundamentalists.

Furthermore, these men were not obscurantists or iconoclasts. Kuyper said it was un-Calvinistic to limit Calvinists to reading only safe books. God in his sovereignty can use the scholarship of unregenerate men to his glory. Machen's mother objected to his going to Germany as it was the seed-bed of liberalism. In one of his most famous letters Machen replied that unless he could meet liberalism head-on, on its own terms, in its own territory, he could not hold his faith in integrity. He furthermore added in another essay that contrary to so many fundamentalists he did not think that all the current critical materials being published were but chaff to be discarded. Lecerf said that any critical statement made about Scripture by a competent nonevangelical scholar had to be taken with great seriousness by the evangelical.

The contemporary evangelical wishes to stand in the same tradition. He seeks to defend his faith without being defensive. He believes that truth will eventually prevail, and therefore he does not fear the openness of scholarship. He is honest with his doubts, and he agrees with Luther that faith without doubt is not faith. He agrees with the Swedish theologian Aulen that faith means conflict.[17]

The modern evangelical believes that the fundamentalists were right in affirming that there is a core of Christian doctrines which if surrendered is the surrender of the Christian faith as historically understood. The claim of fundamentalists that the liberals did not have a right to the name *Christian* is valid, if by Christian, continuity with the historic theology of the church is meant.

However, the modern evangelical has a greater appreciation for the evangelical theologians of the preceding decades that have just been discussed. They saw the issue with more clarity than the fundamentalists. They knew historical theology, and they knew liberal theology far better than the fundamentalists. Therefore their criticisms of liberalism were more trenchant and their defense of evangelical theory more cogent. But they were one with the fundamentalists in affirming that the liberal theologians had so reinterpreted the Christian religion that their version of Christianity was something different than what the church had believed before.[18]

NOTES

1. Friedrich Schleiermacher, *The Christian Faith,* trans. H. R. Makintosh and J. S. Steward (Edinburgh: T. & T. Clark, 1928), p. 52. Italics omitted.

2. Kenneth Cauthen, *The Impact of American Religious Liberalism* (New York: Harper & Row, 1962), pp. 10–11. I will enlarge Cauthen's theses for purposes of clarity.

3. Schleiermacher, *Christian Faith,* p. 183. Italics mine. His extended treatment of the supernatural is found on pp. 70 ff., 178 ff.

4. In my book, *The Pattern of Religious Authority,* I give a critique of the position of religious liberalism at this point, pp. 73 ff.

5. When a leading liberal Los Angeles preacher was asked on a radio broadcast where Hitler would be in the world to come, he answered that he would be in heaven but way down on the ladder.

6. Compare the following: Stewart G. Cole, *The History of Fundamentalism* (Hamden, Conn.: Shoe String Press, 1931); Norman F. Furniss, *The Fundamentalist Controversy* (Hamden, Conn.: Shoe String Press, 1963); Louis Gasper, *The Fundamentalist Movement* (New York: Humanities Press, 1963), contains more about the second generation fundamentalists; Willard B. Gatewood, Jr., ed., *Controversy in the Twen-*

ties: Fundamentalism, Modernism, and Evolution (Nashville: Vanderbilt University Press, 1969), see "A Note on Secondary Sources," pp. 444 ff; Ernest R. Sandeen, *The Origins of Fundamentalism* (Philadelphia: Fortress, 1968).

7. In my work, *The Christian College in the Twentieth Century* (Grand Rapids, Mich.: Eerdmans, 1963), chap. 4 reviews Kuyper's career.

8. See Furniss, *Fundamentalist Controversy,* "Characteristics of Fundamentalists." I have already indicated some of the liberals' treatment of fundamentalists as well as citing Thielicke's observation.

9. James Orr, *The Christian View of God and the World* (Grand Rapids, Mich.: Eerdmans, 1947), pp. 24, 382. See also Thomas Torrance, *Theological Science* (New York: Oxford University Press, 1969). This book attempts to show that unless we reinstate the objectivity of theology in a technological society the credibility of Christianity is a lost cause.

10. Orr, *Christian View of God and the World,* p. 46.

11. Compare the thorough exegetical work in James Denney, *The Death of Christ* (Chicago: Inter-Varsity, 1904); Leon Morris, *The Apostolic Preaching of the Cross* (Grand Rapids, Mich.: Eerdmans, 1955). Unfortunately so many books on the atonement never get down to the hard data of word studies and exegesis of particular texts.

12. Orr, *Christian View of God and the World,* pp. 299–300.

13. B. B. Warfield, *The Plan of Salvation* (Grand Rapids, Mich.: Wm. B. Eerdmans, 1955), pp. 46–47. Italics mine.

14. B. B. Warfield, *Biblical and Theological Studies* (Nutley, N.J.: Presbyterian and Reformed, 1952), p. 5.

15. Ibid., p. 6. Unfortunately, Warfield looked upon higher criticism as a passing phase in the church. Given enough time the Scriptures would be vindicated. His inaugural address at Western Theological Seminary (7 June 1893) was very doctrinaire and did not really come to terms with the seriousness of biblical criticism. See Warfield, *The Inspiration and Authority of the Bible,* 2d ed. (Nutley, N.J.: Presbyterian and Reformed, 1948), pp. 419 ff. Furthermore, Warfield's intensive studies in the witness of Scripture to its own inspiration suffer to a certain degree from "funnel vision" and need to be supplemented by the kinds of materials found in Gottlob Schrenk's article on *graphē* in Kittel and Friedrich, *Theological Dictionary of the New Testament* 1:742 ff. A recent contemporary effort to come to terms with criticism and theology in a positive manner is Roy A. Harrisville *His Hidden Grace* (Nashville: Abingdon, 1965).

16. See Ned Stonehouse, *J. Gresham Machen: A Biographical Memoir* (Grand Rapids, Mich.: Wm. B. Eerdmans, 1955), pp. 336 ff.

17. Gustaf Aulen, *The Drama and the Symbols* (Philadelphia: Fortress Press, 1970). See chap. 2, "The God of Faith."

18. The issues of the controversy at the theological level, and the outcome in church practices and missionary work, has not been stated better than in the work of Charles Harris, *Creeds or No Creeds? A Critical Examination of the Basis of Modernism* (New York: E. P. Dutton, 1922).

Chapter Seven

AN EVANGELICAL APPRAISAL
OF NEOORTHODOXY

Section 24: The emergence of neoorthodoxy

Why could neoorthodoxy be a theological Samson and bring down the temple of liberal theology when all the flailings of the fundamentalists and all the erudite criticisms of the evangelical theologians could not?

Neoorthodoxy was originally called dialectical theology because it set forth theology in paradoxes, as suggested by Kierkegaard. It was also called crisis theology, indicating God's judgment on all of man's works (the meaning of the Greek *krisis* is judgment) and the necessity of a crisis in man so that he will turn to God. In America, neoorthodox theology was first called realistic theology because it attempted to state the sin of man in much stronger terms than did liberalism. It has also been called neo-Reformation theology because it found in the Reformers the most valid version of Christian theology in the history of the church. But the term that has stuck the longest is *neoorthodoxy*.

The term *orthodoxy* indicates in a most general way the wish to keep the faith of the church of the past centuries. It is *neo* in that it wishes to preserve the advances of the Enlightenment and not be stuck with some of the impossible positions of classical Protestant orthodoxy.[1]

The question is then: Why were the neoorthodox so successful in their attack upon liberalism whereas the attack of both the funda-

mentalists and the evangelicals was relatively ineffectual? I suggest
the following reasons:

*The men who led the fight against the reigning liberalism of the
late nineteenth and early twentieth centuries were men trained in
liberalism by liberalism's leading theologians.* Men like Barth, Brunner, Tillich, and Bultmann were trained by the great liberal leaders
of Germany such as Harnack and Herrmann. Harnack's famous book,
What Is Christianity? (given as popular lectures in 1899–1900), is
considered by many the purest and finest expression of the essentials
of liberal theology. William Herrmann (1846–1922) is not well
known in America, but he was a charismatic lecturer in the heritage
of Ritschl. He exerted an enormous influence on Bultmann and Barth.
Barth said that when he started his ministry in Geneva his theology
was none other than that of Herrmann.

Criticism from those trained within a camp or a school or a movement is always far more devastating than criticism from an outsider.
It was one thing for a fundamentalist who might have taken a course
or two at some liberal seminary to criticize liberalism or for a man
like Orr who could read all the German liberals in German to criticize liberalism. It was totally and radically different when men
trained in the bosom of liberalism by liberalism's best teachers turned
upon their mentors and radically criticized their theology.

*Certain historical events caused the neoorthodox thinkers to re-
think their liberalism.* For example, when Barth read the program of
Kaiser William II and saw that many of his liberal professors had
signed it, he said to himself that if these men were so blind to the
demonic in this program there must be something very sick with their
theology. Or, Barth claimed he had an intuition in 1916 that revelation was of grace. If it is truly of grace, then it can only be given of
God. If revelation can only be given of God, then the whole of liberal
theology was built on sand. Barth did not see the full implications of
his intuition at the time, but the rest of his academic life was spent
in working out these implications.

Although sometimes neoorthodox theologians deny that world
events helped shaped their theology, nevertheless the coincidences
of event and shift in theology are remarkable. The period in Western
history when mankind was supposed to have been the most optimistic
about its future was from 1890 to 1914. With the beginning of World
War I a number of national and international tragic events followed
one after another. World War I was so devastating to optimistic

thought because it was man's most catastrophic war. Deaths due to combat and the war conditions ran into the tens of millions. It was fought by the most civilized nations with terrible weapons of technology (tanks, machine guns, airplanes, "Big Bertha," lethal gas). This was followed by the Great Depression, which in turn was accompanied by the rise of ruthless dictatorships, which in turn led to World War II. The problems of slums, intercity decay, organized crime, and gangsterism added to the gloomy picture. What else could theologians do but wonder if they had too easily modified the traditional doctrine of human depravity?

Any doctrine of sin written in the context of such events which did not do justice to the terrible character of these events must be judged as superficial.

The philosophies of idealism which were popular in Germany, England, and America began to melt away as philosophies based on science began more and more to supplant them. The crucial factor was the enormous growth of the sciences in the nineteenth century. Idealism did not really know how to absorb science creatively and meaningfully into its structure. It thus defaulted to the newer philosophies such as positivism, materialism, naturalism, pragmatism, and realism.

All the great liberal theologies were based on some version of philosophical idealism. When idealism was discredited, ignored, or replaced, then liberalism was a system without a foundation. It became an intellectual orphan. Evidence for this is found in Newman's *The Idea of a University* (1852). Newman complains that the philosophers and theologians were being either pushed to the side or crowded out of the universities by the influx of a new breed of professors—the scientists!

This meant that a viable theology of the twentieth century had to be supported by other than idealistic philosophy. It was not that idealism collapsed at once or that idealism has not persisted in philosophy until now. But in terms of percentages, the philosophers of scientism grew larger and larger in proportion to the philosophers of idealism. However, most of the important theologians of the twentieth century turned to other theological options such as existentialism, phenomenology, analytic philosophy, or process philosophy.

A new cultural mood was in the making. Schopenhauer and Nietzsche were declaring the death of a great cultural synthesis and the beginning of a new post-Christian civilization. Kierkegaard was radically reinterpreting the nature of Christian theology and the existential character of the leap of faith. Dostoevsky was writing his *Notes from the Underground* as well as his great psychological novels dramatizing the pathology of the self before Freud. In 1918 a German schoolmaster named Spengler published *The Decline of the West*. To him, Western culture was an elderly animal about to die, preparing the way for a new order. Freud was writing shocking things about infants ("infant sexuality"). Rather than being babies sent from heaven and trailing clouds of glory, Freud saw them as greedy little emotional sponges which, if frustrated, would become neurotics and psychotics.

Just as idealism had a hard time adjusting to science, so did liberalism have a hard time adjusting to a cultural climate which was so contradictory to its assumptions, especially about the goodness of man, the benevolence of God, and a soft line on the doctrine of sin.

Liberal theologians generally accepted the axiom that a higher critical view of Scripture was a mandate for liberal theology. But some scholars did not accept this axiom. I have already mentioned the biblical realists and the holy history school who did not think that the critical assessment of Scripture was a mandate for liberal theology. Biblical criticism and biblical theology could go hand in hand. The origin or composition of a document did not necessarily negate or invalidate its message.

This is essentially the position of Barth and Brunner, although Barth is far less prone to accept the validity of critical judgments than Brunner. Both agree, however, that how a document was composed does not negate its witnessing or kerygmatic character. It meant then that theology could accept the essential conclusions of biblical criticism without accepting a liberal theology as the theological counterpart to biblical criticism. Unexpectedly in book reviews, in particular, scholars who accept the central findings of biblical criticism and nevertheless treat the text with theological seriousness are called conservatives (for example, Eichrodt).

There has been a revived interest in biblical theology. Perhaps the greatest monument to this new interest is Kittel and Friedrich, editors, *Theological Dictionary of the New Testament* (projected nine volumes).[2] All the major words of the Greek New Testament are given thorough historical studies (classical Greek, Hebrew Old Testament, Greek Old Testament, interbiblical rabbinic literature, and patristic literature). The journal, *Interpretation,* is essentially a journal of biblical theology, and it has experienced more than twenty-five years of successful publication. The series, *Studies in Biblical Theology,* systematically keeps putting out new volumes until now it has created a small library in biblical theology. It is also remarkable how the presses have published so many popular, semipopular, and technical commentaries both as series and as individual volumes.

Theologically this is not of one piece. Some of it is even more radical than the older liberal publications. But it does reveal how seriously Holy Scripture is (yet) taken at high academic levels and in real Christian scholarship.

Some things are the preconditions to great events, and other things spark them off. Historians cannot always tell one from the other. Did the situation make Martin Luther, or would the Roman Catholic situation have muddled through if there had been no Luther? We have attempted to set out the preconditions as to why neoorthodoxy was first able effectively to attack liberalism and then to establish itself. The factors that favored the first reenforced the second.

Certainly it was Barth's genius, Brunner's fire, and Bultmann's massive classical learning that sparked neoorthodoxy into prominence. These were no ordinary men.

What is harder to assess but must have been a factor were the changes going on in the Roman Catholic church. The Roman Catholic church was beginning to come to serious terms with Holy Scripture at the turn of the century with the formation of the Biblical Commission. More and more Roman Catholic scholars began to participate in the higher levels of biblical criticism and the writing of commentaries. In America, Roman Catholics have their own biblical journal, the *Catholic Biblical Quarterly.* They have produced their own encyclopedia of biblical theology, *Sacramentum Verbi.* Their scholars are members of, learned contributors to, and officers in the international society of Old Testament scholars and the international society of New Testament scholars. The famous translation, the Jerusalem Bible, is a tribute to the monumental biblical learning now prevailing in the Roman Catholic church. The rejuvenation (*aggiornamento*) of the Roman Catholic church in biblical studies and in theology is certainly part of the story of the success of neoorthodoxy.

Theology has moved beyond neoorthdoxy with such new theologians as Ebeling, Fuchs, Robinson, Moltmann, Cobb, and Pannen-

berg. But our next problem is to give an evangelical assessment of
neoorthodoxy. We shall focus on its best representatives, Barth and
Brunner.

Section 25: The evangelical response to neoorthodoxy

For purposes of discussion we shall take as the basic corpus of
neoorthodox theology the writings of Barth and Brunner. Bultmann,
Gogarten, and Tillich pulled far enough away from Barth and Brunner not to be classified strictly as neoorthodox. Unexpectedly, neoorthodoxy appeared as a St. George, slew the dragon, and wrote a
new Golden Legend. What were evangelicals to think of this? They
had tried to do the same thing but with very limited success. Were
they to be received as brothers in the Lord or as a party yet within
the liberal camp having a brawl with other liberals?

*This was no problem to the fundamentalist who classified all Prot-
estant theologies as fundamentalist or liberal.* The neoorthodox were
neoliberals. Their words may have sounded orthodox, but their doctrines were not. Further, one's fellowship is an indication of where
one's heart is. Neoorthodox theologians mixed with the liberals and
not with the fundamentalists, and that in itself was a giveaway of
their neoliberalism which they mislabeled as neoorthodoxy.

At the level of seminary theology the pace was set for branding
neoorthodoxy as really neoliberalism by Cornelius van Til's book,
The New Modernism.[3] The importance of this book was immense.
What the fundamentalist had sensed was now affirmed and docu-
mented by an accredited theologian. It is van Til's judgment that for
all the apparent orthodoxy of the neoorthodox they are not orthodox
but liberals, for they have not challenged the basic assumptions of
liberalism. Upon inspection, their so-called orthodox doctrines are
not orthodox at all. It is not neoorthodoxy but neoliberalism or, as
van Til called it, the new modernism.[4]

The belief that Barth was on the road back to orthodoxy, however, persisted, and van Til has written a small library on the subject. In one of these works, *Has Karl Barth Turned Orthodox?*
(1954), van Til replied with a resounding no! Van Til concludes his
small book by stating that he is not assessing Barth's eternal salvation, but theologians do have the right to assess the theology of other
theologians. After mentioning the times of the great affirmations of
orthodoxy with their refutations of heresy as Nicaea, Chalcedon,

Dort (where Calvinism was vindicated against Arminianism), and the assembly of the Westminster divines, van Til concludes:

> No heresy that appeared at any of these was so deeply and ultimately destructive of the gospel as is the theology of Barth. Never in the history of the church has the triune God been so completely and inextricably intertwined with his own creature as he has been in modern dialectical thought.[5]

The opposite of van Til's assessment would be to urge that in the truest and most historic sense of the word Barth is orthodox. With genius ability Barth has restated the old faith, the historic Christian theology, in a way that is believable for modern man. Labels are always bothersome and may be ponderous, but I would label this approach evangelical neoorthodox. I would include in this camp such men as Gollwitzer, Otto Weber, Cochrane, and Thomas Torrance. Otto Weber's *Grundlagen der Dogmatik* is considered on the continent one of the most thorough works on systematic theology of our generation. The biblical and historical coverage is immense. Thomas Torrance has not only given us an excellent historical introduction to Barth in his work *Karl Barth: An Introduction to His Early Theology: 1910–1931,* but he has written his own illustrious introduction to theology in his work, *Theological Science.* Barth himself has said from the public platform that his theology is orthodox if by orthodox one means a serious attempt to be in communion with and in continuity with the great theological tradition of the Christian church.

A third reaction among men who profess to be evangelical (for I am intentionally excluding the opinion of men who do not consider themselves evangelicals) *is dialectical.* To react uncritically with a theologian is to accept every line he writes as gospel truth. To react negatively to a theologian is to attempt to shred everything the man writes. To react dialectically is to read a theologian and assess, evaluate, judge, weigh, criticize, approve, and so on. The theologian should not be read with adoring eyes as some Roman Catholic scholars read Thomas Aquinas, seeing no errors, blunders, or mistakes. Neither should the theologian be read through spectacles of pure prejudice so that nothing he says can be trusted or taken at face value.

The evangelical who reads Barth dialectically is just as ready to grant Barth one point as to criticize him at another. This means being very hard on Barth when he clearly drifts away from historical evangelical positions but applauding him when he scores a point. Obviously, each evangelical who reads Barth dialectically differs enormously in what he accepts and what he criticizes. For example, Gordon Clark (*Karl Barth's Theological Method*) grants Barth the minimum, but he applauds Barth for taking liberalism apart and showing that it is not Christian theology. I presume one of Barth's most diligent translators, Geoffrey Bromiley, reads Barth dialectically. Klaas Runia has written *Karl Barth's Doctrine of Scripture,* and although he believes that Barth comes short of the Reformed version of Scripture, he nevertheless says that Barth has many important things to say about revelation, inspiration, and Holy Scripture. This is a dialectical reading of Barth.

Perhaps the biggest surprise in evangelical scholarship with regard to Barth has come from G. C. Berkouwer of the Free University of Amsterdam. Barth had so many unkind things said against him by the very orthodox Dutch Calvinists that he likened them to cannibals and butchers—very strong language![6] But one day the continental bookstores were filled with G. C. Berkouwer's *The Triumph of Grace in the Theology of Karl Barth.*[7] Here was a calm, accurate, fair, and positive appraisal of the theology of Karl Barth.[8] When Barth read it, it almost reduced him to tears, and he confessed that he had to retract some of the harsh things he had said. Furthermore, he paid Berkouwer the scholar's compliment by taking his criticisms seriously and in a succeeding volume attempted to answer them.

Section 26: Elements of value in neoorthodoxy for evangelical theology

Just an an intelligent evangelicalism cannot ignore the Enlightenment as if it had not happened, neither can it pretend neoorthodoxy never existed. The only alternative is to read neoorthodox literature dialectically. At certain points neoorthodoxy has not broken with the presuppositions of liberalism and has given a historic doctrine a novel twist of which the evangelical cannot approve. The evangelical can, however, learn from neoorthodoxy.

Barth tells a humorous story on himself. A young, very orthodox Lutheran pastor wished to converse with Barth, but at the same time he wanted to protect the purity of his stance as an unimpeachable orthodox Lutheran. When Barth greeted him at the door, the young pastor told Barth that he wished to talk with him but that it was not to be construed as an approval of his theology since he was an orthodox Lutheran and not a Barthian. Barth then replied, "Come right in! I am not a Barthian either!"

The point is we do not read Barth to become Barthians but to learn how theology should be written. What Barth told the young orthodox Lutheran was that how one wrote his theology was more important than to what school a theologian belonged. One should approach neoorthodoxy with this dialectical attitude. I have read both the Barthian and Brunnerian corpus of writings. I shall cite Barth more than Brunner because I am more at home with his writings and much of what he says runs parallel to Brunner's thoughts. Just as I attempted an assessment of the Enlightenment as antievangelical as it was, so I shall attempt an evangelical assessment of neoorthodoxy. The following are some of the positive gains in neoorthodoxy which I think are beneficial for evangelical theology:

The evangelical can appreciate the neoorthodox attack upon religious liberalism and use some of its ammunition for his own theology. I have already indicated why Barth, Brunner, and others were able to bring down the house of liberal theology whereas neither the militant fundamentalists nor the learned evangelical scholars could do so. Working with their massive knowledge of historical theology and the history of philosophy, they could pull down pillar after pillar from within. Unfortunately, much of what Barth says against liberalism is scattered throughout his huge volumes, and the present indexes are very inadequate. (Fortunately there is the promise of an index volume to Barth with an English translation so that this logistic problem will be greatly relieved.)

At this point I shall give some sample criticisms that Barth makes of liberalism:

(1) Although modernism attempted to be scientific and critical in the manner in which it wrote theology, it nevertheless failed. It failed because it lost the source, the content, and the critique of all theology: the Word of God. Without that, liberalism had no formal principle whereby to organize its theology.[9] By the expression *the Word of God* Barth does not mean immediately the Scriptures (although that is later brought into the picture) but God as the speaking God in contrast to man as the religious quester.

He adds a further observation. In that preaching in America is so divorced from Holy Scripture (the witness to the Word of God),

Barth does not expect his theology to be appreciated in America. But there is hope! If American Christians ever tire of sermons based on religious topics because they are stupid and stale, then Barth thinks his theology might get a hearing! [10]

(2) The preaching of modernists is empty preaching. Schleiermacher, the great founder of religious liberalism, speaks of the Word of God, but upon examination this turns out to be nothing more than the spirit in all men. If this is the case, there is no real proclamation of the Word of God. Barth so comments: "Modernist thought hears man answer [that is, responds to the words of the preacher] without any one having called him [that is, through the Word of God]. It hears him talk to himself." [11] Preaching in religious liberalism then is merely religious men speaking about religious topics but not preaching in the sense that the Word of God comes from the Scripture through the sermon to the people.

(3) The Christology of religious liberalism is a fantastic oversimplification. To modernists, what is in Jesus is "the revelation of the deepest and final reality of man." [12] This is in sharp contrast to biblical Christology. To Barth the name *Jesus* means "the simple once-for-all reality of Jesus Christ. The Word or the Son of God became a Man and was called Jesus of Nazareth; there this Man Jesus of Nazareth was God's Word or God's Son." [13]

(4) Liberal theology is essentially rank individualism in that each liberal thinks his way to his own synthesis of Christian theology. Barth lists seven such species of liberalism. But a theologian is a theologian in the church, and the church by definition is where the Word of God is spoken. Therefore, theology, to be truly Christian, must first hear what the church has preached and taught as the Word of God, as the gospel, and as Christian theology. When the theologian has heard the word of the church, then he may begin his own theological writing. When liberal theologians do nòt first listen but start writing, they write not the theology of the Word of God but personal opinion.[14]

(5) Because liberals rejected the Holy Scriptures as the controlling, normative source of Christian dogma and the critic of all dogma, they did not advance theology beyond the Reformation. This is an unusual and powerful charge against liberalism.[15] It means that as far as real theological progress is concerned liberal theology simply marked time.

(6) According to Barth, the foundation of biblical ethics is the command of God. The right God makes the right commands, and the authoritative God has the right to make moral commands or he would be less than God. But liberalism constructs a philosophical ethics, thereby creating a subdivision of natural theology. Natural theology to Barth is anti-Christ. The ethics of liberal theology is then a nonbiblical and therefore non-Christian ethics.[16]

This is a sample of Barth's critique of liberalism. A significant contribution to theological scholarship would be a book in which Barth's assaults on liberalism scattered throughout the *Church Dogmatics* (and Brunner's works could be included in this too) would be brought together and set out systematically. It is true Barth later modified some of his earlier more violent statements against liberalism and liberal theology. The older he got, the more sympathetic he seemed to become toward the great liberal theologians of the nineteenth century. For example, he admits that he got from Schleiermacher the idea of a scientific Christian theology in which all doctrines would be coordinated around one central concept.

Evangelical theology should be grateful to Barth for these attacks on liberal theology. Whatever may be irritating in Barth's *Church Dogmatics* should be balanced by what supports evangelical theology against liberalism. It would certainly be shortsighted if the fundamentalist and evangelical prejudice against Barth were so irrational that they could not profit from Barth's assaults upon liberal theology.

The evangelical can appreciate the neoorthodox summons to Holy Scripture as the source and authority of Christian theology (sola scriptura). Although Brunner has a very loose view of Scripture for evangelicals, Brunner does not believe that there is encounter and salvation without doctrine, and that doctrine must come from Holy Scripture. No fundamentalist statement of the authority of Holy Scripture in the church is stronger than Barth's when he says that the authority of the Scripture in the church is direct, absolute, and material.[17] All other authorities in the church—a remark aimed at the Roman Catholic and other orthodox groups—are indirect, relative, and formal.

Certainly liberalism did use Scripture and did give it special status in the church, but it did not give it binding authority in theological assertions. The authority of Scripture rested more in its moral insights, its purified view of God, and the kinds of religious experi-

ences it promoted. But Barth and Brunner are solidly behind the
sola scriptura of the Reformers when it comes to the theological
status of Scripture.

When it comes to the use of Scripture in theology, Barth has used
more Scripture than any other theologian in the history of theology.
He does this three ways: (i) Barth uses all the important theological
passages of Scripture known as "seats of doctrine" and comments
extensively on them. (ii) In discussing a number of topics Barth
makes his own concordance of all the relevant passages on the topic.
(iii) At critical points he has devoted many pages to exegesis. Some
of these are so extensive and valuable they have been extracted and
printed as separate little volumes.

Evangelicals have been unhappy with Barth's overall view of
Scripture. The best evaluation and critique of Barth's view of Scripture is Klaas Runia's *Karl Barth's Doctrine of Holy Scripture*. Barth
is right in assuming that the highest point of revelation, namely the
incarnation (John 1:14), should be the point of departure for the
construction of a doctrine of revelation and from that of Scripture.
But having said that, the problems begin. Barth's favorite expression
about the nature of Scripture is that it is a witness to revelation. Here
is one of the sharpest points of conflict between most evangelicals
and Barth. Evangelicals believe that Scripture is directly revelation,
not merely a witness to revelation. Coming at it from another direction, Scripture is indirectly the Word of God to Barth; whereas to
evangelicals it is directly the Word of God.

Barth also differs radically with evangelicals on what inspiration
is. To Barth, inspiration is the willingness of the writers of Scripture
to be witnesses of revelation. To evangelicals, inspiration is the process whereby the revelation or Word of God is cast into written form.
Barth takes the *theopneustos* of 2 Timothy 3:16 in a subjective
sense: It expresses the psychological state of the writers of the Scripture. Evangelicals take it in an objective sense: It indicates the divine
activity which produces a divine product, namely, Holy Scripture.[18]
Warfield has shown that words with an *-eustos* [19] ending are active
words indicating what is produced rather than the process of producing.

Due to the massive reconstruction of a doctrine of revelation by
neoorthodox theologians and an almost equal underplaying of the
doctrine of inspiration, inspiration as a theological topic has practi-
cally disappeared from theological discussion. Only evangelicals and

fundamentalists, as well as some Roman Catholics, are keeping the concept alive.

Evangelicals are also unhappy about the neoorthodox view of the humanity of Scripture. The assumption is that only men of the same order can communicate with each other. Infallible angels cannot really communicate with fallible men nor can, as the neoorthodox reason, infallible men communicate to fallible men. Therefore, for Scripture to communicate it must be written by fallible men. This is the humanity of Scripture. If human, then it must contain error, for to be human is to be fallible and therefore to err.

The concept of the humanity of the Scriptures can be found in Luther and Calvin if by humanity one means accommodating revelation so that man may comprehend it. Calvin likened God speaking to man to a nurse training a child to speak. In the nineteenth century Kuyper paid great attention to the worldly or cosmic character of revelation. But to none of these men did the humanity of Scripture or its worldly character or its cosmic dress imply that of necessity Scripture must contain error or lose its divine character. If there is error in Scripture, it is an empirical fact and not a necessity growing out of the accommodated character of revelation.

Finally, evangelicals are not happy with Barth's allegorical [20] interpretation of Genesis 1–3 which makes creation a christological concept or sets the concept of creation within the covenant of grace. Allegorical interpretation has not been popular with evangelical theologians due to its abuse in past historical epochs, and they are not happy about any attempt to revive it.

Regardless of these shortcomings, evangelicals see in the neoorthodox view of Scripture the wish to restore theological dignity to Scripture which liberal theology took away from it. With all their qualifications about Scripture, Scripture is nevertheless to Barth and Brunner the one written authority in the church. It is over all councils, traditions, definitions of the papacy, or opinions of the Fathers.

Evangelicals appreciate the return of the neoorthodox theologians to the Reformers, not only to Luther and Calvin, but to lesser men as Melancthon, Bucer, Zwingli, Vermigli, and so on. Barth and Brunner were in a quandary when they rejected their liberal theological heritage. To return to Protestant orthodoxy was not possible because they were children of the Enlightenment as much as the liberals, regardless of their high estimation of the older orthodoxy. Who would they own as their fathers?

They found the Reformers to be more congenial to their way of thinking than any other group of theologians before or after the Reformation. Barth and Brunner both became steeped in the writings of Luther and Calvin. Both men did study the theologians before and after the Reformation, but the drummer they heard was the drummer of the Reformation.

Barth has the most extensive discussion in Protestant theology over the question: who are our Protestant fathers? [21] After surveying the options he maintains that the fathers of the modern Protestant theologians are the Reformers. This discussion of "Protestant Fathers" is another one of the unusual surprises in *Church Dogmatics*.[22] Barth is very harsh with the liberal theologians, asserting that their wandering away from the mainstream of Christian theology was a waste of time.[23]

Evangelicals are with Barth in finding our nearest of kin, theologically speaking, among the Reformers.

Evangelicals appreciate the neoorthodox interaction with the whole history of theology. Both Barth and Brunner attempt a real historical coverage as they develop their theologies. Some theologians believe that when Barth turned to theology the church lost its greatest historian of theology. Because Barth has written more extensively than Brunner, he has more historical materials. Unfortunately Barth is not consistent in his methodology. For some doctrines he gives a sum of the whole development of the doctrine since patristic times. With other doctrines one would not know a word had ever been written before Barth wrote he so completely ignores the historical materials. Regardless of this unevenness of development, Barth has not only the greatest amount of Scripture in his theology of any theologian, but he has the most historical theology.

One of Barth's criticisms of the ecumenical movement is that the present leaders of it think only of conversing with the living! To be truly ecumenical the living must converse with the dead through the medium of historical theology. Evangelicals who with Calvin have their own version of the indefectability of the church, and have their conviction of the teaching ministry of the Holy Spirit, also want to be conversant with theologians of other centuries.

Evangelicals are especially in debt to Barth for his detailed criticism of Roman Catholic theology. Brunner does give some space to this phase of theology but nothing like Barth does. If there should be a volume in which all of Barth's antiliberal materials are collected, there should also be one on his anti-Catholic utterances.

Here, as with liberalism, the problem is that the materials about Roman Catholic theology are spread all through the *Church Dogmatics*. At one point Barth attacks its Marian theology, at another point its theory of ethics, and at another point its idea of tradition. His most massive attack is launched against the Roman Catholic theory of natural theology based on the philosophical doctrine of the analogy of being. Historically Roman Catholic theology has taught that man by his own reason, unaided by grace or the Holy Spirit, can prove the existence of God, natural law, the immortality of the soul, and the divine origin of the Roman Catholic church. This ability to reason from the natural order of things to divine truth is based on the assumption that the Creator leaves traces of his nature in what he creates, the analogy of being. (I trust the reader learned in philosophy will pardon the effort to state a very complicated matter in such a simple manner.) One of the strongest things Barth has ever written has been about Roman Catholic natural theology based on the analogy of being (Latin: *analogia entis*). On this subject he writes: "I regard the *analogia entis* as the invention of Antichrist, and think that because of it one can not become Catholic." [24]

Barth was too sick to attend Vatican II, but when he was able to travel, he did go to Rome. Upon reading the Vatican II documents, he registered his criticisms in terms of sharp questions reported in the small book, *Ad Limina Apostolorum* (a title taken from the piety of the Middle Ages when the pilgrims to Rome had come to the boundaries of the apostles, for according to Roman Catholic tradition both Peter and Paul died at Rome).

Here again the point is not to become Barthian, but to ignore Barth's massive criticism of Roman Catholic theology would be an unwise act by an evangelical theologian.

The evangelical can greatly enrich his own understanding of theology and especially of historical theology by a diligent study of the massive writings of Barth and Brunner. I repeat: Barth and Brunner must be read dialectically. One should not remove his critical spectacles when he reads these men. But they were men of immense learning who took the historic doctrines of the church with great seriousness. Certainly it is significant that some claim there is a greater Roman Catholic literature on neoorthodoxy than Protestant. It is because these men lived with historical theology and historical topics. They may not defend the evangelical version of a given doc-

1THE EVANGELICAL HERITAGE

trine, but an evangelical who will put himself through these materials will, in that process itself, give himself a theological education. The few hours theological seminaries alot to theology represent a very meager education in theology compared to putting one's self through the huge volumes of Barth and Brunner.

The fear of many evangelicals and fundamentalists is that this is a risk. How can a person read these men without being converted to their theology or being pulled out of the evangelical orbit? The plain truth is that there is no education without risk. If a school indoctrinates, it does not educate. Furthermore, carefully controlled indoctrinated teaching may create radical rebellion rather than conformity. Furthermore, the student not exposed to nonevangelical options in an evangelical atmosphere is an easy prey to a nonevangelical option offered in other circumstances. Play the game any way you want. You cannot eliminate risk. Yes, there is risk in the serious study of Barth and Brunner. But serious risk in any discipline is the price of real scholarship, so if we want the scholarship we have to run the risk.

To show that I do not read these men without critical assessment, I will indicate certain areas of disquietude I have with neoorthodox theology. The ability to be objective about any theology is one of the means of lowering the risk in the study of that theology:

(1) I am unhappy with the general antipathy of Barth and Brunner to Protestant orthodoxy and evangelical theology. Of the two, Brunner is the more outspoken and caustic. Some of the accusations Brunner makes against orthodoxy and fundamentalism in *Revelation and Reason* are certainly extreme and uncalled for.

There is an element of truth in the fundamentalists' claim that the people one fellowships with is more indicative of the real intention of his theology than the words he writes. Barth and Brunner have hardly made the Bible conference circuit!

(2) I am unhappy with the imbalance in neoorthodoxy in terms of the amount of space given to revelation as over against the very little space given to inspiration. Barth understands inspiration as the willingness of the prophet to be a witness to revelation. This hardly measures up to the biblical data on inspiration. Barth's view of Holy Scripture might have been far more impressive and durable if he had given as much energy to investigating inspiration as he did revelation.

(3) Van Til's mass of anti-Barthian materials is not to be bypassed because one thinks he systematically misinterprets Barth.

Barth's great passion is to make the wall of time that separates the witness of Holy Scripture of God's action in the past from the present fall down or become so transparent that that very Word of God is heard by modern man. The danger in such retranslation is that the new concept is not a faithful version of the older one but its betrayal. This is van Til's major concern, and therefore before any assent is given to a neoorthodox version of a doctrine, one must ask if the original biblical substance is retained.

(4) Barth is a Christomonist, and it is to be questioned if all of Scripture can be given a christological interpretation. A Christocentrist believes that Christ is the center of Scripture, the center of theology, and the center of the gospel. I am a Christocentrist. But Christomonism is Christocentrism carried to the extreme. To Barth there are not two covenants: one in creation, and one in redemption. There is only one covenant of grace. God's covenant of grace in Christ tells me the meaning of the great cosmos in which I live; the great cosmos in which I live is the theater of the drama of redemption. This forces Barth to an allegorical interpretation of some of the Old Testament so as to assume creation under grace. It eliminates the concept of general revelation, for if there is only a covenant of grace, then there is only one kind of revelation—soteric or special.

(5) Liberalism taught that wrath is the disciplinary side of God's love. The wrath of the God of traditional or historic theology was unloaded for a theology of the monism of love in which wrath is but a species of love. I must seriously question whether Barth has really broken with the liberal tradition of the monism of love and fails to see the wrath of God as it is revealed in Scripture. Of course, a monism of love makes serious inroads into the concept of the holiness of God. Such a monism of love must refine the holiness of God. A God of a monism of love may find sin distasteful and even repugnant, but he cannot hate it with that hatred born of the perfection of moral rectitude which I think is the God of Holy Scripture.

(6) Barth's monism of love makes me restless with his doctrine of the atonement.[25] In many ways Barth offers correctives to the liberal view of the atonement and seems to teach real suffering in God for man's sins. But at certain critical points Barth backs away, for example, at the point of punishment. For all the objectivity which Barth seems to put in the cross, has he not already undermined that objectivity by his Christomonism and his monism of love which together really eliminate any substantial attribute of wrath in God?

(7) Barth is a situation ethicist. His version of situation ethics was so academic, however, that it did not make the impact of Fletcher's *Situation Ethics*. Barth vigorously opposed Hitler and the Nazi party and had a major hand in writing the Barmen Declaration.[26] But Barth took a trip to Hungary and Czechoslovakia and came back making no such angry noises against communism. When he was called inconsistent, he replied that he could only be inconsistent if he followed an ethics of principles. In such an ethics an act could be assessed as contrary to principle. But Barth replied that he does not govern his ethics by principles but by situations. Therefore he claimed that there was no contradiction in his opposing the Nazis who were willfully trying to corrupt the Christian gospel and not opposing the Communists who clearly let it be known that they were enemies of the church. In my book, *The Right, the Good, and the Happy,* I take issue with situation ethics. Ethics without principles is a contradiction in terms, and I oppose Barth's situation ethics as much as I oppose Fletcher's even though Barth does not bolster his case with the notorious kind of cases Fletcher uses.

In summary, neoorthodoxy is to be read dialectically. To read Barth or Brunner uncritically is to be trapped in all of their errors. To read Barth and Brunner in a spirit of total negativism is to impoverish one's knowledge of theology. To read them dialectically is to have the good without the evil and to separate the error in the quest for the truth.

NOTES

1. For historical coverage of the emergence of neoorthodox and related theologies, see: Thomas Torrance, *Karl Barth: An Introduction to His Early Theology* (Naperville, Ill.: Allenson, 1962); Henri Bouillard, *Achievement of Karl Barth* (New York: Herder & Herder, 1957); James Robinson, ed., *The Beginnings of Dialectic Theology,* trans. Keith R. Crim and Louis De Grazia (Richmond, Va.: John Knox, 1968); Boniface A. Willems, *Karl Barth: An Ecumenical Approach to His Theology* (Paramus, N.J.: Paulist/Newman, 1965); James Smart, *The Divided Mind of Modern Theology, Karl Barth and Rudolph Bultmann 1908–1933* (Philadelphia: Westminster, 1967); Rudolph Bultmann, *Existence and Faith: Shorter Writings of Rudolph Bultmann,* trans. Schubert Ogden (Cleveland, Ohio: World Publishing, 1960).

From an abundance of recent works on contemporary theology, I suggest that the best guide is William Nicholls, *Systematic and Philosophical Theology,* ed. R. P. Hanson (New Orleans, La.: Pelican, 1970).

Many special neoorthodox terms I have defined in *A Handbook of Contemporary Theology* (Grand Rapids, Mich.: Eerdmans, 1966). This book also gives alternative definitions of the same terms by different theologians. The list of abbreviations (pp. 139–41) is also a functional bibliography of neoorthodox literature.

2. See O. Betz, "History of Biblical Theology," A–D:432–37, and K. Stendahl, "Contemporary Biblical Theology," A–D:418–32, *The Interpreter's Dictionary of the Bible* (New York: Abingdon, 1962).

3. Cornelius van Til, *The New Modernism* (Philadelphia: Presbyterian and Reformed, 1946).

4. Both Barth and Brunner claimed that they did not recognize their theology in *The New Modernism.* Van Til was more dialectical in his critique than they ever intended to be in their theology. T. F. Torrance takes the new modernism apart piece by piece in a scathing review in the *Evangelical Quarterly* (1947) 19:144–49. Apart from the numerous inaccuracies of interpretation, Torrance makes the point that if van Til's method is turned back on van Til, one can prove van Til heretical several different ways, using van Til's own dialectic against him.

5. Cornelius van Til, *Has Karl Barth Turned Orthodox?* (Philadelphia: Presbyterian and Reformed, 1954), p. 181. Van Til has produced a great deal more material on Barth and neoorthodoxy in books, articles, and book reviews.

6. C.D. IV/2, p. xii.

7. G. C. Berkouwer, *The Triumph of Grace in the Theology of Karl Barth* (Grand Rapids, Mich.: Eerdmans, 1956).

8. In an appendix, "The Problem of Interpretation," ibid., Berkouwer is very sharp with van Til, saying that van Til violated the first rule of scholarship in assessing another person's theology. Van Til has not accurately understood or represented Barth's theology and should be called to task for it.

9. C.D. I/1, p. 288.

10. Ibid., pp. 291–92.

11. Ibid., p. 68.

12. C.D. I/2, p. 12.

13. Ibid., p. 13.

14. Ibid., p. 830.

15. Ibid., p. 660.

16. C.D. II/2, pp. 520 ff.

17. C.D. I/2, p. 538.

18. Evangelicals derive their interpretation of 2 Tim. 3:16 from Warfield's exhaustive study, *Inspiration and Authority of the Bible,* pp. 3–70. Unfortunately, Barth apparently was unaware of Warfield's thorough research.

19. There is a Greek lexicon in which the words are spelled backwards so that a scholar can readily deduce the meaning which suffixes or particular endings give to words.

20. Paul does call the Abraham-Sarah-Hagar relationship an allegory (Gal. 4:24). Historical research has shown that the word *allegory* did not have the special meaning to Paul that it did for later interpreters. Even if it were an allegory in the later sense, it could be an *ad hominem* argument against the Judaizers and, therefore, not a hermeneutical rule for the interpretation of Scripture.

21. C.D. I/2, pp. 585 ff.

22. Ibid., pp. 603 ff.

23. Ibid., p. 660.

24. C.D. I/1, p. x.

25. C.D. IV/1.

26. The text of the Barmen Declaration is found in the Presbyterian Book of Confessions.

Chapter Eight

EVANGELICAL THEOLOGY IN THE RIGHT PERSPECTIVE

Section 27: Evangelical theology seen askew

Any philosophy or theology or political theory should be judged by the works of its best expositors, not by its poorest. This is what the evangelical wants done with evangelical theology. There is literary trash in any tradition, and no reflective member of that tradition wishes his thinking to be represented by the trash. When evangelical theology is measured by the trash in its tradition, it is seen askew. Because in so many instances evangelical theology is judged by its poorer literature, certain criticisms of it have become routine. In order for evangelical theology to be seen in its best light, some of these misconceptions must be corrected.

In essence evangelical theology is not obscurantistic. Obscurantism is ignoring or rejecting knowledge or denying its claim to truth. The evangelical does not wish to avoid responsible criticism. But he does not believe a responsible criticism would lead one to judge evangelical theology as obscurantistic.

The evangelical theologian does not intend to be an obscurantist. He has no intention of crucifying his intelligence. He wishes to make a clear distinction between that which he thinks is rational and sensible criticism of his opponents in contrast to the irresponsible attacks of the obscurantists. The evangelical cannot deny that there are evangelicals and fundamentalists who are obscurantists. The point is that being an obscurantist is not part of the essence of being an evangelical.

The evangelical believes that the tradition in which he stands is not an obscurantistic tradition. Can one say that Augustine or Thomas or Anselm or Luther or Calvin or Edwards was an obscurantist? There is no second way to truth other than the way of solid scholarship. Evangelicals may at times be hesitant to agree to the latest theory, but that is born out of much experience when the latest theory has been gladly received only later to be unmasked as an error.

There is a justification for a spirit of hesitancy among evangelicals. To them Holy Scripture is the Word of God, and therefore matters of biblical criticism are to be taken with maximum seriousness. A scholar who has no such conviction is more willing to accept a new theory and more ready to reject an older theory for the newest. The seriousness with which the evangelical takes the doctrine of inspiration does not allow him to hang loose about comings and goings in biblical criticism.

The same situation prevails in science. The evangelical knows that facts are facts, that truth is truth, and that reality is reality. He cannot by thought or will dissolve facts, truth, and reality into nothingness. He is not therefore an obscurantist with reference to science. But again the seriousness with which he accepts Holy Scripture as God's revelation makes him hesitant about accepting every new proposal in science simply because it is the latest. It is not obscurantistic to attempt to be just as careful with one's biblical data as one is with one's scientific data. Obscurantism occurs when science or knowledge is irrationally or emotionally rejected because it seems on the surface that certain claims are contrary to Scripture. For example, when Michael Polanyi (*Personal Knowledge*) and Langdon Gilkey (*Religion and the Scientific Future*) attempt to show the prescientific assumptions which make science possible, or show the nonscientific elements introduced in scientific theory, they are not obscurantists. They are apprehensive of scientists uncritically making scientific knowledge an absolute, overlooking how much nonscientific assumptions are behind the scientific method and how much nonscientific plastic surgery must be done with any scientific theory to round it out.

Although the direct equation of God and Truth comes out in Neoplatonic philosophy, it is a tacit assumption of Holy Scripture. In the Old Testament there is a persistent witness that the Lord of Israel is the one true and living God; that all his words are truth; and that all he does is truth. A similar witness in the New Testament centers around Christ and the gospel. Christ himself is the Logos and the Truth; the gospel is the Word of truth. The Gospel of John reveals as no other book in the New Testament the passion for truth. This biblical passion for truth shows that in principle biblical theology cannot be obscurantistic in the presence of the biblical concern for truth. Concern for truth does not prove that one's concerns are true. That, however, is not the issue. The issue is attitude, and the biblical concern for truth expresses an attitude toward truth which shows that the stance of the Scripture itself is against obscurantism.

In essence evangelical theology is not a literalism. One of the most frequent charges of the nonevangelical theologian against the evangelical is that he is a literalist. This matter of being literal or nonliteral is more complicated than the comments suggest.[1] Historically the word *literal* has been used in contrast to the word *allegorical.* Within this context all nonevangelicals are literalists in their method of biblical interpretation. It is synonymous with grammatical or philological interpretation. If this is the meaning of *literal,* then all Protestant scholars who follow the usual grammatical or philological method in their interpretation of Scripture are literalists.

On the other hand literalism may really mean letterism. By letterism we mean the failure of the interpreter to differentiate prose from other literary genre and figures of speech in Scripture; or that verbal inspiration requires that all the Scripture be interpreted as if it were prose. An example of letterism is Fritz Braun's *Das dreistöckige Weltall der Bibel.* Braun takes all the figures of speech and all the literary genre in Scripture which describe creation as if they were all unvarnished prose statements. He creates for us a fantastic picture of the cosmos with his kind of letterism and says that if his findings disagree with scientists that is too bad for the scientists. He states that if one must choose between the divine Word of God in Scripture and the human word of man in science, the Christian will take the divine Word of God in Scripture.

It is unfortunate that nonevangelicals confuse literalism with letterism. The competent evangelical interpreter is no more a letterist than is the nonevangelical. In fact, the shoe may be put on the other foot! Seeking the "Word behind the words" or the "existential kerygma" within the myths of the New Testament or searching for the "symbol" or "image" behind the prose might be modern sophisticated versions of allegorical interpretation.

The evangelical scholar is not a "wooden-headed literalist." He knows the species of literary genre and the traditional figures of speech; and furthermore he knows that these occur in Holy Scripture; and accordingly he interprets them for what they are and not with a grinding literalism. He feels that the charge that he is a naïve literalist is not true, and, more than that, such letterism is not of the essence of evangelical theology.

Another charge against evangelicals which is closely associated with that of literalism is that the doctrine of inspiration held by evangelicals drives them to a flat view of the Scriptures. By a flat view of Scripture is meant that if all Scripture is inspired (plenary inspiration) then all parts are of equal importance. This, so the charge goes, forces the evangelical to take some incidental event of the Old Testament or trite observation in the Book of Proverbs with the same seriousness as John's Gospel or a Letter of Paul's. Evangelicals do not hold a flat view of Scripture. It does not follow that if all Scripture is inspired all is equally important. Some passing observation in Ecclesiastes is not on the same level of theological importance as John 3:16.

It is true that in previous centuries when theologians had no sense of the progressive character of revelation that they would cite some obscure Old Testament passage as having as much weight in establishing a doctrine as some clear statement in the New Testament. But the modern evangelical does not handle Scripture that way. He is aware of the progressive character of revelation; of the degrees of importance of the different parts of Scripture; and of the necessity of never using a passage of Scripture in proof of a doctrine without being sensitive to its location and function in Scripture.

Being reactionary or quietistic or exclusively personal or conservative in ethics is not of the essence of evangelical theology. There are some segments among evangelicals that suggest this. When religious liberalism made so much of the Social Gospel and ridiculed personal salvation as religious selfishness, the strategy of many fundamentalists and evangelicals was to ignore the Social Gospel and stress personal salvation. It was a position taken not from the essence of evangelical theology but as one of the many attempts to counteract religious liberalism.

Further, there are those who believe that conservative religion gives theological vindication to conservative politics and economic theory. Conservative political and economic views are individualistic to the degree that they wish to distance themselves from socialism or creeping socialism or more and more government control of business and industry. But here again the essence of evangelical theology does not call for a reactionary policy in politics and economics, or a quietism in the face of social evils, or that conservative theology is the proper religious base for conservative views in economics or politics.

That the Christian church suddenly awoke to social awareness and responsibility late in the nineteenth century is not true to the facts. The concept of *corpus Christianum,* deriving from the Emperor Constantine, demanded that the church be in the political, economic, and social life of the empire. The fact that this relationship was capable of corruption, even gross corruption (for example, E. R. Chamberlin, *The Bad Popes*), does not efface the fact that the church was not intended to be a purely self-enclosed religious institution. Further, the idea of a Christian civilization and the debates over the concept of a Christian civilization revealed a belief that somehow the church was to minister to the total population as well as to itself. The idea that the church was the conscience of the state, or that the church was the cultural-producing society in the state, also shows that the church had a social responsibility. Luther's doctrine of two kingdoms was a large part of his social ethics (although not all of it). The Reformed doctrine of common grace meant that the church must participate in civic, cultural, and educational concerns with non-Christians.

The set of conditions created by the Industrial Revolution precipitated the Social Gospel. The terrible working conditions, city slums, and the desperate status of the poor drove the liberal theologians to the Social Gospel. The promotion of the Social Gospel in contradiction to personal salvation in turn caused many evangelicals to overemphasize personal ethics and shy away from social ethics because it would make them appear to have become liberal in their theology. All of this is unfortunate. Sometimes with short steps and sometimes with longer strides the evangelicals of today are trying to reaffirm their social ethics. Any person familiar with certain evangelical Christian periodicals, certain evangelical denominations, and certain evangelical interdenominational youth evangelistic movements knows that social ethics is a red hot evangelical issue. There is a real generation gap between the old evangelical who formed whatever social ethics he had by reacting to the Social Gospel and many of the young evangelicals who insist that Christians as persons and Christian churches must participate actively in the social revolution now in progress in America. They demand that passion for evangelism and missions must be matched by a passion for social justice. They insist that the doctrine of redemption (salvation by personal faith in Christ) must not efface the doctrine of creation (the order of justice and morality for all men) and its passion for social justice.

Regardless then of some of the unhappy alliances of conservative theology with conservative politics and economics, it is not of the essence of evangelical theology to reduce Christian ethics to purely personal ethics for Christians only.

The essence of evangelical theology does not presume that the final or near-final statement of Christian theology has been achieved. Evangelicals and fundamentalists have yielded to the temptation to identify their theology as if it were virtually identical with the faith of Jude 3 ("once for all delivered to the saints") and the unchangeable Christ of Hebrews 13:8 ("the same yesterday, today, and forever"). If this is the case, then any deviation from their theology is a deviation from the very truth of God itself. That is a most serious charge.

The evangelical believes in growth within a tradition. Credit must be given to John Henry Newman who wrestled with this problem in his famous work *Essay on the Development of Doctrine* (1845). His task was to show that the simple church of the Book of Acts and the complex Roman Catholic church of the nineteenth century were the same church. He attempted to show by what criteria a theologian could identify real growth as separate from mere change or deviation. His basic thesis is that the church of the Book of Acts grows within a controlled tradition into the present very intricate and complex Roman Catholic church. A very interesting evangelical attempt to interpret the idea of development from the evangelical perspective is the essay of Peter Toon in *The Reformed Journal,* March 1973, entitled "The Development of Doctrine."

The opposite of growth within a tradition is development away from the tradition. As indicated earlier, religious liberalism was not growth within the mainstream Christian tradition but a development away from it. The confusing thing is that both processes are going on in the church at the same time: growth within the tradition and development away from the tradition.

Although we may not concur with Newman's particular theses, in general he is right. The church is not to be theologically static.

Evangelicals believe that the church should grow theologically, but this growth must be within the bounds of tradition, that is, within the limits which define Christianity as historically understood. Evangelicals and nonevangelicals divided fundamentally at the concept of what growth in theology means. One of the reasons evangelicals lose a steady trickle of their ministers and scholars to various versions of nonevangelical theology is that these young students and pastors do not clearly understand the difference between growth within a tradition and deviation from a tradition. They think that their only alternatives are to stay in the theological rut of their early fundamentalism and stagnate or jump to some recent nonevangelical theology and keep in the center of the modern theological action.

Growth in tradition takes many forms. For example, it may mean a new interpretation of such a classical passage as Romans 5:12–21. Perhaps the Adam-humanity, Christ-church parallel needs restatement. Or, it may mean a new interpretation of the great incarnational passage of Philippians 2:4–11. Perhaps we must come to some evangelical version of a kenotic Christology. But such changes in exegesis will be growth within the evangelical tradition.

Growth may mean rejecting an older model in theology. Much American fundamentalism and evangelicalism has been influenced by federal theology, stemming principally from J. Cocceius (1603–69). In this theological model, Adam and Christ are federal figures, each representing humanity. More recent biblical theology speaks of corporate personality as the concept which expresses unity by the biblical writers. This could mean that evangelicals must shift their traditional model of a federal headship to one of corporate personality—a topic which may be further researched in Aubrey R. Johnson's famous little book, *The One and the Many in the Israelite Conception of God,* as well as the concept of Adam as humanity in G. A. F. Knight's *A Biblical Approach to the Doctrine of the Trinity.* It is true that evangelicals believe they have a stable theology stemming from a stable tradition, but it is not the essence of evangelical theology not to grow within the bounds of its theological tradition.

It is not of the essence of evangelicalism to believe that revelation is solely propositional or only the conveying of information.[2] It is a scholarly scandal how many contemporary nonevangelical scholars accuse the whole evangelical camp of believing in propositional revelation or revelation as the mere communication of truth thus sapping from it all its biblical dynamic. However, this attack on propositional revelation rarely discusses how a nonpropositional revelation can give rise to books loaded with theological propositions by theologians who deny propositional revelation. If a farmer declares that a cow is dry, and yet milks a bucket of milk from the cow, he is certainly using the word *dry* in an odd way.

It is true that some evangelicals have said that revelation is propositional. The issue is not whether some evangelicals have said this, but whether it is part of the essence of evangelical theology. Extreme breeds extreme. When neoorthodox and existentially oriented theologians deny propositional revelation and assert that revelation is only confrontation with God or a divine-human encounter, then the evangelical pushes to the other extreme and declares all revelation is propositional. Both alternatives are false.

If there were no conceptual elements in revelation, there could be no theology. In principle both Barth and Brunner admit this when they affirm that the Scriptures are a witness to revelation (and therefore somehow organically connected to it else they could not be witnesses) or that Christ and the gospel cannot be present apart from doctrine (for then the doctrine must somehow come out of the revelation in order to make revelation "come off"). No theologian can perform the miracle of deriving conceptual elements from a revelation that is purely nonconceptual, that is, the pure presence of God.

How could Barth write thirteen immense volumes of theology plus the hundreds of lesser titles contained in the bibliography in *Antwort* if revelation were completely free from the conceptual or propositional? How could Brunner write his several extensive monographs and then his three volumes of dogmatics if revelation were totally free from the conceptual or propositional? When Barth and Brunner blast the evangelicals amidst their mountains of books of their own writings that revelation is not conceptual or propositional, what more appropriate reply can an evangelical make them than a bemused smile?

On the other side of the ledger, the evangelical tradition has always had its witnesses that while revelation may be in words it is also in the divine Presence; it is something spiritual as well as rational; it is confrontation as well as speaking.

Luther believed that revelation was more than a matter of words.

It was the Holy Spirit who took the historical Jesus out of the past and made him a present reality to faith, and it was the same Spirit who brings the heavenly Christ down to the believer so that he is aware of the presence of his Lord. In the opening pages of the *Institutes of the Christian Religion,* Calvin repudiates any barren intellectualism with reference to faith in God but insists that all true religion is accompanied with piety. The witness of the Spirit,[3] developed in detail by Calvin, eventually became part of the theology of the Lutheran, Reformed, and Anglican churches. This doctrine prevents the Scriptures from becoming a dead book or a mere book of religion or a helpless book of the law. The doctrine of the illumination of the Spirit in the experience of regeneration became a standard topic in Protestant orthodox theology. Furthermore, the insistence of the Reformers that faith was primarily trust (*fiducia*) and not merely assent (*assensus*) to the truth of the gospel added a further dynamic element to their theology. If one reads widely enough, he will discover a number of preneoorthodox theologians in the evangelical camp who interpreted revelation as much as the divine Presence or the divine Confrontation as they believed revelation to be a disclosure of truth.

Furthermore the evangelical recognizes a number of literary figures of speech in Holy Scripture (simile, metaphor, hyperbole), as well as literary genre (biography, poetry, aphorisms, letters, autobiography, parable, and apocalyptic imagery), all of which are not direct, immediate prose assertions and therefore not in the form of propositions. Revelation does come in these nonpropositional forms. There is appeal to imagination in Scripture as well as to mind, and we certainly know that imagination far more powerfully affects the self than conceptual thinking.

However, the evangelical believes that in revelation there is a maximum concern for truth, or in theological language, for a valid knowledge of God. He fears that in the current emphasis on revelation as encounter, or revelation as an existential communication, or revelation as the divine Presence, or revelation as an existential speech-event, that this seriousness for truth is lost and the reality of the knowledge of God is lost. And it logically follows to the evangelical that if these are lost theology as a discipline with a real content, a real object, a real subject matter is also lost. Theology topples down to the same level as philosophy and becomes an endless series of attempts to express one's ideas about God or religion in

some more current or more revolutionary or unexpected way. There
is no real progress or deepening of man's understanding of God;
only restless change. Therefore, if the evangelical is overly emphatic
about revelation being propositional, this is what is in the back
of his mind.

*In essence evangelical theology is not anticultural, world-denying,
or inherently pessimistic.* Because some evangelicals have thought
culture to be composed of the devil's sophisticated pastimes, and
that the world is evil and should be shunned, and that because man
is sinner we can expect only the worst from society, some nonevangelicals have presumed that these attitudes belong to the essence
of evangelical theology.

The evangelical does believe from revelation given in Scripture that there is an inherent "Christ against culture" in all culture.
Paganism is always a possibility in world history. Further, the
evangelical knows that the world does have corrupting elements in
it. There is not only ballet but also burlesque; there are not only
honest games of sport but betting rackets around the sport, and so
on. The evangelical does believe that culture can never escape the
destructive elements of sin, and viewing culture purely as the City of
Man, the evangelical can have only a pessimistic attitude toward its
moral future. But this is the realistic application of the strong biblical
doctrine of sin, and those who do not see things this way have not
measured the full weight of sin.

Unfortunately in America fundamentalism is taken for orthodoxy.
There is, however, another more positive, more affirmative, and
more creative tradition.

In his illumination theory of knowledge Augustine saw all truth
as originating in God, sacred or secular, and therefore the Christian
was in deep obligation to the truth of God as discovered by non-
Christians. The medieval theologians did not violently oppose creation to redemption but said that grace does not contradict nature
or creation but perfects it and completes it. This is a far more
healthy attitude toward creation, culture, and history in spite of its
possible theological problems than the contemporary fundamentalist's
separation of them. Unfortunately, the extreme emphasis in fundamentalism on redemption inadvertently greatly weakens its doctrine
of creation.

Luther has been accused of being a violent antirationalist. He did
write:

> But the devil's bride, reason, the beautiful harlot, comes in and acts smart. Whatever she says she considers she said by the Holy Spirit. Who can help here? Neither lawyer, doctor, king, nor emperor. This devil's whore is the worst of all. The other crass sins are noticed but reason is judged by no one.[4]

But Luther also wrote:

> Reason is also a light and a beautiful light. . . . It is indeed true that reason is the principal and most important possession of all. It is above all things of this life the best of something divine. Reason is the inventor and ruler of all arts, medicine, law, and all wisdom, might, virtue, and honor which men can possess in this life. Indeed, reason must be called the essential difference by which man is distinguished from the animals and the other things. Holy Scripture makes reason a ruler over the earth, its birds and fishes and cattle, saying "rule." This means reason is a kind of sin and divinity given for the administration of the things of this life. And this majesty God has not taken from reason after Adam's fall, but rather confirmed it.[5]

Some of the things said of Calvin make one wonder if most persons writing about Calvin ever really read him. It is hard even for scholars to break away from a Calvin-stereotype. Calvin's theses are essentially those of Luther. Reason in sin makes a man proud and defiant of God's truth. Therefore, the supreme virtue of sinful man before God is humility. At this point Calvin begins a discussion of the fact that "man's nature endowments [are] not wholly extinguished [by the fall and sin]." [6] He devotes six very impressive paragraphs to maintain this thesis. The style is so elegant and the language is so clear that anything short of giving the full text itself leaves so much unsaid. I will, therefore, resort to a sampling of his thought.

Although the supernatural gifts of God to man in creation were lost through sin, the natural gifts were not, and enough reason remains in man so that man is to be distinguished from beasts. Sin could not "completely wipe out" reason for "some sparks still gleam" in man. Nor did man's will utterly perish. Then Calvin makes the following remarkable comment:

> For we see implanted in human nature some sort of desire to search out the truth to which man would not at all aspire if he had not already savored it. Human understanding then possesses some power of perception, since it is by nature captivated by love of truth.[7]

Next he states that man is a social creature and all men have within themselves "universal impressions of a certain civic faith dealing and order" and it is these seeds which give rise to specific laws for man knows "law and order" before he is ever taught it. The seeds of law have "been implanted in all men." The conclusion that Calvin draws is that if all men have some sense of political order then "this is ample proof that in the arrangement of this life *no man is without the light of reason*" (italics mine).

Next he discusses art and science and finds that the capacity for art and science are gifts of God for all men. They are not natural endowments as if independent from God, but they exist because of God. Calvin regards "the Spirit of God as the sole fountain of all truth." Therefore if we despise art and science—fundamentalists take note!—"we condemn and reproach the Spirit himself," for it logically follows that if the Spirit is the fountain of art and science, to despise art and science is to despise their author, the Spirit.

Calvin then puts in a commending word for ancient jurists, doctors, men of mathematical sciences, and pagan poets. Even though Scripture calls these men "natural men," nevertheless they "were sharp and penetrating in their investigation of inferior things. Let us, accordingly, learn by their example how many gifts the Lord left to human nature even after it was despoiled of its true good." This is not at all in accord with the rantings one finds in so many books which claim that Calvin thought human nature totally depraved and therefore totally corrupt and totally bereft of anything worthy of dignity and respect. This is the difference between the Calvin of caricature and the Calvin of the *Institutes*.

In paragraph sixteen Calvin pushes further his thesis that "human competence in art and science also derives from the Spirit of God." He makes the sharp observation that "if we neglect God's gift freely offered in these arts, we ought to suffer just punishment for our sloth." Finally he speaks of the general grace of God as the source of all reason, science, art, and learning. He concludes that "we still see in this diversity some remaining traces of the image of God, which distinguish the entire human race from the other creatures." [8]

This concept of the general grace of God has been developed by later Reformed theologians into the systematic doctrine of common grace.[9] It is called common because it is, in Calvin's word, general, that is, it applies to all men, unregenerate or regenerate. It is called grace because man has no right to it. By sin man has forfeited all. Special revelation, special grace, is that which redeems man. Man shall survive and not devour himself out of existence by his hatreds, nor degenerate into the life of a brute by loss of reason, but shall have a culture and civilization with government, law, education, art, science, and economics. In this God has given all men grace.

Abraham Kuyper has been called the greatest Calvinist since Calvin, and he has pursued this vein of Calvin's thought with force and consistency. For example, in his book on Calvinism he indicates that Calvinism is not just a doctrine of salvation but a total life system involving politics, science, and art. He writes:

> Thus understood Calvinism is rooted in a form of religion which was peculiarly its own, and from this specific religious consciousness there was developed first a peculiar theology, then a special church-order, and then a given form for political and social life, for the interpretation of the moral and world-order, for the relation between nature and grace, between Christianity and the world, between church and state, and finally for art and science.[10]

What Kuyper says of art is also important in showing that evangelical theology has a world-affirming dimension that so frequently gets dropped out in its exposition. Kuyper writes of art as follows:

> As image-bearer of God, man possesses the possibility to create something beautiful and to delight in it. This artistic ability is in man no separate function of the soul but an unbroken (continuous) utterance of the image of God. . . . Understand that art is no fringe that is attached to a garment and no amusement that is added to life, but a most serious power in our present existence, and therefore its principle variations must maintain, in their artistic expression, a close relation with the principle variations of our entire life; and since, without exception, these principle variations of our entire human existence are dominated by our relation to God, would it not be both a degradation and an underestimation of art, if you were to imagine the functions, into which the art-trunk divides itself, to be independent of the deepest root which all human life has in God? [11]

There is a corresponding limited pessimism in evangelical theology, and this again is due to its inherent serious doctrine of sin. The evangelical believes in *amelioration* (things may be made better) but not in *utopia* (things may be made perfect). These ideal states that philosophers, politicians, and even theologians have dreamed about from Plato's *Republic* to current projections of a future scientific, cybernetic utopia are all betrayed in the very origin of the word *utopia*. It is derived from the Greek word for negation, *ou,* and the word for place, *topos.* Hence, utopia means "nowhere." And the evangelical concurs that utopia (for example, B. F. Skinner's *Beyond Freedom and Dignity*) is nowhere. Human sin and depravity prevent man from ever forming any system of government or creating any body of laws that will eliminate all evil and injustice in human society. In this regard the evangelical is a pessimist, and to date history is on his side.

But he is a limited pessimist because it is God and not man that has the last word. God's kingdom will come. Christ shall return in great power and glory. There will be the new heaven and the new earth in which dwell the new Jerusalem. Scripture ends with the Book of Revelation, and the Book of Revelation ends with the complete revelation of the glory of God and the glorification of man. This is the final and eschatological optimism of evangelical theology.[12]

It is also felt that the evangelical has a cruel and provincial attitude toward non-Christian religions and the great non-Christian peoples of the world.

The issue here must be clearly stated. If a theologian does not accept the Great Commission of the New Testament, or the necessity of personal salvation, or the reality of the wrath and judgment of God, then his assessment of the evangelical's missionary attitude is a matter of profound theological differences and not a critique of the evangelical's attitude. We simply have to confess we part company at profound theological points.

To the contrary, the evangelical does not believe he can be faulted for his evangelistic and missionary theology. He believes the love of God is undifferentiated. He does not believe he belongs to an inner circle of love that in principle excludes all non-Christians and pagans. The evangelical does not believe he is in any way superior to peoples of other religions. He is not more intelligent, more holy, more righteous, more religious, or more serious. Whatever the evangelical has of salvation or truth, he has it by virtue of grace.

Every sensitive evangelical is a universalist at heart. He agrees with Peter when he wrote that "the Lord . . . is not wishing that any should perish, but that all should reach repentance" (2 Pet. 3:9). In perhaps that passage of Scripture which represents the sovereignty of God the strongest—Romans 9—God's attitude towards Pharaoh is that he endured him with much patience (Rom. 9:22). The idea that God is as much glorified by the damnation of the lost as by the salvation of the saints as held by some Calvinists is hard to reconcile with Ezekiel 18:23: "Have I any pleasure in the death of the wicked, says the Lord God, and not rather that he should turn from his way and live?"

No person on the face of the earth wants everybody in heaven more than an evangelical. Only an evangelical really knows in depth the meaning of sin, the wrath of God, the reconcilation of the cross, the victory of the resurrection, the tragedy of judgment, and the glory of the New Jerusalem. Every person who fails of this final beatitude can only be of pain to him.

In summary, many of the narrow and restrictive charges against evangelicals are not part of the essence of evangelical theology. There are evangelicals and fundamentalists who believe them. That is not denied, but it is also not the point of the debate. The point of the debate is that these beliefs and practices are not of the essence of evangelical faith and therefore not characteristic of all evangelicals. Taking a cue from Schleiermacher, I have tried to say that the cultured and educated despisers of fundamentalism and evangelicalism may be despising matters not of the essence of original, authentic Christianity. If they could shed their misconceptions, they might find the way of faith now hidden to them behind a pile of unnecessary brambles.

Section 28: Contemporary divisions among evangelicals

As I indicated at the beginning of this book, my definition of an evangelical is a very broad one. This means that evangelicals as sinners have had, do have, and will have serious differences among themselves. There is no sinless perfection in theology merely because one professes to be an evangelical. Just as regeneration is not glorification and leaves much of the "old man" in us unchanged, so regeneration is not the glorification of the intellect. It too is subject to the corrosive influences of sin. Therefore, evangelicals do have differences, yes, even sharp and bitter differences. Let us take a brief look at some of the contemporary ones:

(1) There are still some ardent Calvinists and some ardent Arminians in the evangelical camp, and from time to time they renew their ancient feud. Furthermore, there are still theologians

and pastors who believe their denominational distinctives with a vengeance and consider it part of their sacred calling in life to defend the absolute biblical foundation of the ecclesiology of their denomination—even when they are antidenominational!

(2) The question of the millennium has cooled off in recent decades, but we still have a strong premillennial group among the dispensationalists. It would not be amiss to say that the assumption behind the great creeds and confessions of the Reformation was amillennialism. The Lutheran Augsburg Confession of 1530 did condemn the premillennialism of the Anabaptists based on Jewish eschatology. The sharpest eschatological conflict in America is between the dispensational premillennarians and the Reformed amillennarians. Postmillennialism has lost much of its appeal because the twentieth century saw mankind headed more obviously toward some sort of hell on earth than a glorious reign of the church. However, there is a disguised postmillennialism in both process theology ("we are headed for the Omega point") and the theology of hope ("we are headed for the *novum* and more and more *utopias*").

(3) Perhaps the sharpest division of the decade among evangelicals has been over the nature of inspiration and inerrancy. There are three ingredients to this controversy, but they are not always plainly brought to the surface; hence, the controversy persists in having fuzzy edges. (i) One group of evangelicals believes that the most strategic doctrine evangelicals have against modern nonevangelical theologies is the inerrancy of Scripture, whereas the other group thinks that a total apologetics which includes a doctrine of Scripture is the position of strength. (ii) One group of evangelicals thinks that inerrancy means that all statements of fact, or simply all statements of Scripture, are without error (with due regard to literary genre), whereas the other group believes that the church has always put a limitation on the authority of Scripture by saying Scripture is the final or supreme authority in matters of faith (doctrine) and practice (morals, ethics). (iii) One group of evangelicals approaches the doctrine of the inspiration of the Scriptures by exegeting all the verses that define the nature of inspiration and then learning to live with the problems of the Scriptures, whereas the other group believes that the entire nature of Scripture ("the phenomena of Scripture") is as important in framing a doctrine of inspiration as is the exegesis of particular verses.

(4) The problem of Christian liberty, or the *adiaphora,* "indiffer-

ence," controversy, is still with us. One group of evangelicals believes in a code-ethics. This means drawing up a list of the evils in our present society (card-playing, dancing, drinking, and so on) from which all Christians should abstain. Others believe that no Christian and no church have a right to bind a Christian's conscience where Scripture does not bind it. Therefore, in such secondary matters of culture (the *adiaphora* or indifferent things) each Christian has the freedom to do as he pleases as long as he respects the conscience of other Christians and does not confuse the unbeliever.

(5) Evangelicals are divided on the strategy of combating modernism and other nonevangelical theologies within their own denominations. The separatists believe that the denominations are apostate and that to remain within them is to create terrible theological confusion, especially in missionary work. Therefore, the only possible strategy for an evangelical is to leave the denomination and form a new one based on biblical theology. Others believe that the denomination is their denomination, and they do not wish to surrender it to the modernists. If the denomination forces them out or evicts them, then that is another matter.

(6) The Bible-and-science issue is not dead. One group of evangelicals believes that, in the main, scientists are on the right track and it would be foolish to contradict modern science or indict modern science as a whole. Biblical interpretation must always be done with one eye scanning a textbook of science. The other group believes that unsaved man will oppose God's truth at all levels, and this includes science. Evangelicals must never, then, bend their interpretation simply to concur with the latest science. Furthermore, there are periodic outbursts against evolution either in journal articles, books, or protests against the teaching of evolution in the public school system as if it were a scientific fact and not a speculative theory.

(7) There is a charismatic movement among evangelicals that is dividing them. Speaking in tongues, healings, mystical experiences, and other unusual spiritual phenomena are occurring among small groups within the major denominations. There is the tacit assumption among these evangelicals that evangelical theology is overrationalized which robs the Christian of power and that denominational machinery chokes off the freedom of the Spirit. On the other hand other evangelicals believe that the charismatic movement cannot stand the test of real biblical interpretation. It is a psychological or

sociological phenomenon and not the real workings of the Holy Spirit.

(8) There is a generation gap among the older and the younger evangelical ministers. The older group wants things preached the way they used to be preached; evangelism and missions done the historic and customary way; and church music still to consist of "the great hymns of the church." The younger ministers are much more aware of psychology, counseling, and therapy groups. They are interested more in dialogical preaching than monological sermonizing. They think the evangelical should be in the midst of social change, social action, and social ferment. Further, they are willing to be far more experimental in church music and methods of worship.

Section 29: Some guiding convictions of contemporary evangelical theology

The evangelical knows that he can only be a contemporary man. He cannot undo genuine progress in science, technology, and learning in general. Any retreat to a safe past in theological literature is a failure of nerve to live in the present. But at the same time the evangelical is not victimized by the modern man. This is an important distinction. The evangelical believes that he must accept all that science and learning have established on a sound basis. But he does not believe that because something is new or recent or mod it is by its very modernity true.

The criteria for writing dependable history are generally agreed upon. Certainly historians cannot go back to moralizing or romanticizing about history. If historians differ, it is over the status of some rule of historiography or the interpretation or the evaluation of some event. This is very different from cultural fads.

The contemporary evangelical is in a unique and difficult position: He believes the divine authority of an ancient document that becomes more ancient with each passing year; yet he knows he can only be a contemporary man. He must live with and in his own generation and its culture. Some of the convictions of this contemporary evangelical and Christian theology are:

The evangelical believes that Christianity is one and not many and is not capable of continuous radical reinterpretation. That an evangelical believes in growth within evangelical tradition has already been affirmed. However, an evangelical believes that there are three alternatives to the problem of change and/or growth in theology.

(1) A theologian may look at religion as primarily a religious attitude or a specific kind of religious feeling, or he may understand that faith as personal response is a constant factor, the same in all ages. But the theologies woven around such a faith come and go with the passing cultures. Theology is accordingly an effort to give some sort of rational explanation or cohesiveness to our beliefs. But one theological system succeeds another endlessly as history continues to unravel.

One is reminded at this point of Herman Hesse's *Magister Ludi: The Glass Bead Game.* It is Hesse's symbolic and sarcastic summing up of Western man's attempt to try to find himself by purely rationalistic methods. The great scholars of Europe invent the greatest and most intricate of all games which takes decades of concentrated learning to master. Hesse calls this *The Glass Bead Game.* Actually, it is an empty, meaningless game from which self-deluded rational perfectionists derive their delight.

The evangelical wonders seriously, not flippantly or superficially, if most nonevangelical theology is but a religious glass bead game.

(2) The various theologies that are constructed in the history of theology and which diverge from Christianity as historically understood are heresies. A heresy means a personal choice as over against the confession of the church. Unfortunately, the heresy of heresies in the twentieth century is to believe that heresy is not possible.

Certainly error is possible in science. It would be unbelievable for an academy of scientists to outlaw the concept of error in scientific theories. The evangelical believes that if there is error in science, there is error in religion. In theology we call it heresy. Why should we get red in the face, elevate our blood pressure, feel the Inquisition descending upon us, or stir up our adrenalin glands if someone says heresy is possible? Is the contour of theology so sloppy, so vague, so indefinable, so indefinite, so nebulous that the concept of error is totally inapplicable?

The evangelical is, frankly speaking, puzzled by theologians who take such an odd view of truth and error in theology which is so contradictory to how they regard truth and error in science and all other areas of human learning, including textual and literary criticism!

(3) Christianity is one; it is the truth; our evangelical theologies are attempts to come systematically closer and closer to the truth. Theology is like science: it is both an activity and a product. Philosophy may be a kind of activity which never arrives at a product by virtue of its function or nature or definition. But science cannot exist only as an activity. It is an activity which seeks a product— laws, generalizations, reliable frequences, dependable periodicities, hypotheses with a high probability. The evangelical sees theology the same way.

"Jesus Christ is the same yesterday and today and for ever" (Heb. 13:8) is not a statement of Christology as usually assumed. The author of the Epistle states the enduring truthfulness of the Christian religion over against the temporality of the Mosaic revelation and the vagaries of doctrine in the Christian community. In our language it says Christianity is one and and not many.

Furthermore, the same Epistle uses the Greek word *hapaks*— "once for all"—as one of its favorite words. The cross is a once-for-all event. It refers to the once-for-all-ness of the Christian gospel and the Christian revelation, again suggesting that Christianity is one and not many.

No doubt fundamentalists have used Jude 3 (". . . to contend for the faith which was once for all delivered to the saints") to mean that God has delivered the fundamentals of Christianity to the fundamentalists and all modern theology is therefore heresy. In spite of the fundamentalists' abuse of the passage, the passage does say something. This verse too uses *hapaks*—once for all. It also uses the technical Greek verb indicating that an opinion or decision or document is officially handed down from the determining body to the secondary body (*paradidomai*). Furthermore it uses the word *faith* (*pistis*) as a noun, indicating a body of teaching and not an attitude of trust. In our language it is saying that Christianity is one and not many.

There is a doctrinal core to Christianity that cannot be negotiated away. We are imperfect and have only a theology of the cross. We do not have a definitive, once-for-all statement of this core with sharp boundaries. But it is the evangelicals' presupposition in their understanding of the character of Christian theology that explains why they are both skeptical about so many modern reinterpretations and find it so hard to interact with a theological world whose concept of the Christian faith and its theology is so radically different.[13]

Evangelical theology is christological and incarnational. The central motif of Scripture which furnishes the principle of organization for Christian theology has not always been keenly felt by the theologians of the church. In *The Biblical Theology of Saint Irenaeus,* John Lawson claims that Irenaeus is the first one to work out such a scheme. It is known as the recapitulation theory. The first man, Adam, and the first woman, Eve, are put through a test and fail, bringing mankind into a state of sin. But the second man or Adam, Christ, and the second woman or Eve, Mary, are put through their test of the cross, and they remain faithful to God. In so doing they achieve salvation. Many Christian schemes of redemption are variations on this theme.

F. W. Dillistone has given us an impressive list of various schemes of redemption held in the church in his work, *The Christian Understanding of the Atonement.* That which shows through all of these theories of redemption (for his book is really more about the larger schemes of redemption than the narrower theories of the atonement) is that the Christian church has attempted to be Christocentric in its doctrine of redemption. The evangelical stands in this tradition.

Barth and Brunner have restressed for our generation the Christocentric theology of the Reformers. It is the avowed intention of both of these theologians to pick up where the Reformers left off and as consistently as possible reconstruct all theology on a Christocentric basis. Although evangelicals believe that Barth and Brunner have used this principle divisively, evangelicals nevertheless want to also stand in the Christocentric tradition of the Reformers. It is this incarnation and Christocentric center of evangelical theology which prevents it from being called cultic. Cultic and sectarian movements are not Christocentric or incarnational centered in their theology, but evangelical theology is no such deviation from historic Christianity.

The evangelical does not believe that the decision to be Christocentric is arbitrary. According to Hebrews 1:1–3, Christ is God's highest and final revelation. If that is true, then all revelation must be oriented around its supreme manifestation. The seven theses contained in Hebrews 1:1–3 about Christ identify him not only with revelation but also with creation, redemption, and consummation. It is the Scripture itself which teaches us to be Christocentric. Furthermore, Christocentrism is only possible because there has been an incarnation. He who was very God of very God became very man of very man existing on this earth under human conditions as the one Lord Jesus Christ.

This Christocentric and incarnational emphasis in evangelical theology makes it continuous with the mainline traditions of Christian theology. Evangelical theology is not cultic. It is not provincial. It is not sectarian. It is not individualistic. It is divisive only as the truth is divisive in all areas of human learning. It is not feckless accommodation to modern man simply to be modern.

The evangelical finds his case stated very well in Harry Blamire's *The Tyranny of Time: A Defense of Dogma.* It is true that in general modern man knows more than Renaissance man, medieval man, or classical man. But to believe that in theology because something is new or recent must by its very recency be true is the tyranny of time. If Christian theology is built on the divinely revealed Word of God, then criteria are operating in Christian theology that do not operate in other areas of knowledge. The test for truth in Christianity is conformity to the Word of God. For the theologian to presume that the latest or most recent is the truest is to fall victim in theology to the tyranny of time.[14]

The evangelical believes that faith is the fundamental response of the sinner to the gospel and is the foundation of Christian experience. Both Romans and Galatians, the most substantial books on the mode of salvation, set faith in the center as that basic and essential response of man to God's promises in the gospel and as man's fundamental attitude toward the Savior, Jesus Christ. Man is justified by faith; regenerated by faith; and continues into sanctification by faith.

When it came to the final authority in religion, the Reformers espoused *sola Scriptura*—only Scripture.

When it came to the sole basis of redemption, they espoused *sola Christus*—only Christ.

When it came to God's attitude, they defended *sola gratia*—only grace.

When it came to how sinners receive the grace of God and Jesus Christ, they said *sola fide*—only faith.

However, faith is not a simple act but a complex one. From one perspective it was trust in the person of Christ; from another it was assent to the truth of the gospel; from still another it was obedience to the Word of God; and yet further it was knowledge of the contents of the gospel.

Faith is also the beginning of love, for faith in Christ results in the love of God being shed abroad in the hearts of believers (Rom. 5:5). If love is the supreme virtue of the Christian life, faith is the initiating virtue of Christianity.

The evangelical who really understands the New Testament doctrine of faith guards it very jealously. For this reason he has strong reservations about a state church of which a person is considered a member and baptized simply because he is a citizen of the state. No one has so mercilessly attacked this weakness in the state church as Kierkegaard, especially in his work *Attack on Christendom.* Even Barth has challenged the right of the canton of Basel (Baselland) to consider all its inhabitants who have not declared otherwise as members of the Reformed church. The evangelical is also highly suspicious of what the Reformation motto, "the religion of the prince is the religion of the people," does to personal faith.

The evangelical is apprehensive not only of situations in which Christianity is so much the custom of the land that personal faith virtually disappears, but also situations in which faith is made too subjective or too highly schematized. He is afraid that existentialism, in its desire to make faith so intensive and transforming, tends to underplay the seriousness of ascertaining the object of faith. God's work for me is always and ever the foundation of God's work in me. Or, with Horace Bushnell, the evangelical is wary of evangelicals who work out a pattern of faith and conversion and demand that all conform to the pattern. This can be the death of that unique element each person brings to his own decision of faith but which is necessary for that person to really believe ("internalize his faith").

The evangelical was apprehensive about the Social Gospel because in the crusade for justice in society the indispensable act of faith in Christ was either omitted or ridiculed as selfish religion. The evangelical is wary of current emphases on social action or political theology for the same reason. The same danger exists as existed with the Social Gospel. Either the summons to repentance and faith in Christ is dropped out of the church's program, or else personal faith in Christ is interpreted as sick, introverted religiosity. The evangelical has no objection to great concern for correcting social, economic, and political evils. More and more evangelicals and evangelical churches are entering into social action. However, the evangelical accepts the New Testament as his divine authority, and that New Testament has a personal gospel that summons men to repentance and faith. Attempts to shake man loose from that faith by name calling ("selfish religion," "Pietism," "religiosity," "introverted piety," "social indifference") should not cause him to blink for one moment about the centrality of faith as taught in the New Testament.

The evangelical believes that theology will have genuine dignity if it retains an important and nonnegotiable element of the objective in its doctrine of revelation. In an effort to get away from the old orthodox view of Scripture, or to get away from the fundamentalists' extreme objectifying of revelation, contemporary theology interprets revelation in terms of encounter or existential communication. But in dropping out of revelation any objective element in terms of historical act or as a revealed divine Word, it has forfeited the academic dignity of theology. What is meant by the academic dignity of theology? In any university of integrity no department can exist without a responsible and justifiable object or subject matter. When existential theology and neoorthodox theology relegate revelation totally to either an internal existential decision or the pure confrontation of God as subject, anything substantial about our knowledge of God that would make it a responsible object or subject matter worthy of a scholar's time, talent, and energy has been evaporated. Fortunately Barth and Brunner have been inconsistent, and revelation in a disguised objective form has been admitted into their theology.

If Barth wishes to call Scripture the witness to revelation, and not *the* revelation or *a* revelation, he has nevertheless tied Scripture into the concept in such a way that Scripture is certainly revelational. And when Brunner says faith in Christ is impossible without a corona of doctrine, that doctrine is certainly revelationally imbued doctrine.

The evangelical believes this is a certain amount of theological double-talk. He would prefer these men to come out and affirm that revelation is polydimensional, and that one of those dimensions is Holy Scripture. This would protect the integrity and academic dignity of theology, and the evangelical wishes to fight hard for this integrity and dignity in a culture that demands high standards of intellectual respectability and critical self-evaluation of what one offers as knowledge for men to accept.

The evangelical believes that the real touchstone of a theology is its spiritual power not necessarily its intellectual shrewdness, or sophistication, or learning. The apostle Paul wrote: "But I will come to you soon, if the Lord wills, and I will find out not the talk of these arrogant people but their power. For the kingdom of God does not consist in talk but in power" (1 Cor. 4:19–20). He also wrote:

"And my speech and my message were not in plausible words of wisdom, but in demonstration of the Spirit and power, that your faith might not rest in the wisdom of men but in the power of God" (1 Cor. 2:4–5).

It is a natural temptation in an academic community to think that the most scholarly works or the most creative hypotheses or the most penetrating insights are the best or the truest. This is as much a temptation in the theological academic community as in the secular academic community.

These two passages in Paul clearly state that the criteria used in ordinary discourse or arguments or debates or oratory do not obtain with the gospel. This is not to belittle scholarship. It is to recognize that the universe of discourse prescribes its own criteria. The doctor who is an expert toxologist and an expert in postmortems may be a very untrustworthy surgeon. People in the performing arts are not expected to have Ph.D. degrees. An expert in art history may be incapable of painting anything but a smudge. In none of this is scholarship belittled, but it is frankly recognized by all informed people that the universe of discourse sets the criteria of judgment.

Paul said that in the realm of the Spirit the criterion was power, and not wisdom, eloquence, or learning. What did he mean by power? Certainly if the gospel is the power of God unto salvation (Rom. 1:16), the first manifestation of the power of a man's message is the ability to make true converts to Jesus Christ. This means in the context of Romans 1:16–17 to bring them to an experience of justification by faith. Or, in the language of John 3 it means that the message preached causes men to be born anew or born from above but, in either interpretation, to undergo a profound spiritual renewal.

The second meaning of *power* must mean the creation of a genuine new life in Christ. Paul calls it "the law of the Spirit of life in Christ Jesus" (Rom. 8:2). In 2 Corinthians 3:17 "the Lord is the Spirit" and he causes Christians to grow from stage to stage ("from one degree of glory to another," v. 18). Or, in Galatians 5:16 it is walking by the Spirit, the result being the fruit of the Spirit (v. 22: love, joy, peace, patience, kindness, goodness, faithfulness, gentleness, self-control).

The temptation of the theological student and pastor is to be impressed by a theology for the wrong reason. Sometimes it is the novelty of a theology that is attractive. Certainly the fusion of the ideas of the Marxist Bloch and biblical eschatology in the theology of hope is novel. Sometimes it is the brilliant learning and thinking as in the theology of Tillich. Or, it may be a brutal frankness which provokes our admiration of the theologian's honesty. (We would want an evangelical theology to have some of these virtues.) We do not reject them as such. We reject them when they are the sole criteria for accepting a new theology and where the question of power is never considered.

Evangelical theology attempts to be a theology of power. It does want the Word, but it also wants the Spirit. It wants exposition, but it also wants application. It wants understanding, but it also wants transformation. It wants academic excellence, but it also wants spiritual excellence. It may lack in academic prestige, but if it is still a religion of power it can easily bear that reproach. Evangelical theology may be charged with having a dated theology, an irrelevant way of stating the gospel for modern man, a crude approach to human psychology, and some inadequate ways of interpreting the Scriptures. It can bear up under all of this too if it still has power.

The nonevangelical with academic polish, learned theology, communication skills, and expertise in religious psychology who is devoid of power is, according to Paul, not "with it" when it comes to the kingdom of God—1 Corinthians 4:19–20!

The absolute distinction between saved and lost still governs the thinking and theology of the evangelical.

From the Book of Acts to the Enlightenment, Christianity was believed in all its major communions to be a religion of redemption or salvation. Furthermore, this redemption or salvation made a real distinction among men, not a relative one. However, with the advent of religious liberalism the distinction between Christian and non-Christian became relative. The wall between church and world tumbled down.

At this point it is very difficult for the nonevangelical to really tune in on the wave length of the evangelical. If being saved or lost is a real distinction among men, then theology takes upon itself utmost seriousness. The evangelical believes that not only are theological issues at stake, but the very substance of his own eternal destiny. Being a Christian is being saved. It is a life style. It is a program of an ethic of love. It is compassion for all the hurts and injustices of mankind. It is a quality of inner life. It is an endeavor to achieve authentic existence and new being. But none of these are at the center.

Because the evangelical still maintains the real distinction of saved or lost and not merely Christian or non-Christian, he cannot shop theologies or review theological options like the person who holds no such conviction. If there is no objective redemption in Christ received and experienced by faith, then the evangelical's understanding of Christianity is destroyed.

If this is the case, it is not a matter of an evangelical finding a better theology, or liking Tillich better than Moltmann, or Pannenberg better than Bultmann. It is more than finding a theology that seems to be consonant with modern science or some brand of contemporary philosophy. The issue before the evangelical is not to be with the latest theology, or with the most scintillating option among contemporary theologies, or to be on the "in" with the theological community. At this point the evangelical is least understood, for his salvation is linked to his theology which is not the case with nonevangelical theologies. And unless the nonevangelical understands this absolute seriousness of the manner in which evangelicals regard what is at stake in theology, the nonevangelical will persistently misunderstand or ridicule or belittle the evangelical. But until the evangelical can be shown that the difference of saved and lost is not absolute, that the difference between the church and the world is not one of a kind, and that Christian and non-Christian represent but degrees of awareness of a heritage, he will still think in terms of saved and lost which in turn will govern the entire way he looks at the theological enterprise.

NOTES

1. I have discussed the problem of the use of the word *literal* and its synonyms in my book, *Protestant Biblical Interpretation* (Grand Rapids, Mich.: Baker Book House, 1970), pp. 119 ff.

2. I have a much larger discussion of this problem in *Special Revelation and the Word of God* (Grand Rapids, Mich.: Eerdmans, 1961), pp. 154 ff.

3. For the historical documentation, see the bibliography in my *The Witness of the Spirit*, pp. 131 ff.

4. Quoted in G. W. Forell, *Faith Active in Love* (Minneapolis, Minn.: Augsburg, 1960), p. 54.

5. Ibid.

6. *Institutes*, bk. 2, para. 12–17. See also Günter Gloede, *Theologia*

Naturalis bei Calvin and Werner Krusche, *Das Wirken des Heiligen Geistes nach Calvin,* chap. 3, "The Gifts of the Spirit for the Maintenance of Human Society."

7. *Institutes,* bk. 2, para. 12.

8. In the use of Calvin, see the excellent help contained in the footnotes of Battle's translation of the *Institutes.*

9. A similar story could be told of the Lutheran and Anglican traditions, but I am purposefully limiting this discussion to the Reformed.

10. Abraham Kuyper, *Lectures on Calvinism* (Grand Rapids, Mich.: Eerdmans, 1931), p. 10. See also Clarence Bouma, ed., *God-centered Living or Calvinism in Action* (Grand Rapids, Mich.: Baker Book House, 1951), contains chapters on education, art, recreation and amusements, political action, economic patterns, business endeavor, social problems, and international relations, as well as a 13-page bibliography on Calvinism and Calvinistic action.

11. Kuyper, ibid., p. 142 fn., 151.

12. In my book, *Them He Glorified* (Grand Rapids, Mich.: Wm. B. Eerdmans, 1963), I have attempted to spell out this final glorification in great detail, tracking down the meaning of each word, expression, and symbol in the New Testament which speaks of that final glorious state of man.

The latest of the utopia speculators is the off-beat Marxist, Ernst Bloch, who has had such a profound influence on Jürgen Moltmann and the whole new school of the theology of hope. To Bloch, utopia hovers always in the future and its ultimate realization remains in question. See Jürgen Rühle, "The Philosopher of Hope, Ernst Bloch," *Revisionism: Essays on the History of Marxist Ideas* (New York: Praeger, 1962), pp. 166–78.

13. No more eloquent statement of the theological confusion created in the life of the church by the liberals' idea that Christianity is many and not one is to be found than Charles Harris, *Creeds or No Creeds? A Critical Examination of the Basis of Modernism* (New York: E. P. Dutton, 1922). He explains how ridiculous it appears on the mission field for an evangelical missionary to tell nationals in one village how to be saved when a liberal missionary is telling the next village that all evangelical doctrines are false.

14. Calvin does not hesitate to call the church the mother of believers —a concept that is patristic in origin and very essential to the Roman Catholic concept of the church. The title of chap. 1 of bk. 4 of the *Institutes* is "The True Church with Which As Mother of Us All the Godly Must Keep Unity." Para. 4 is entitled "The Visible Church As the Mother of Believers." This shows how Calvin wanted to keep the unity and continuity of the church which was his way of escaping the tyranny of time.

Chapter Nine

THE FUTURE OF
EVANGELICAL THEOLOGY

Section 30: Evangelicals must be students of Holy Scripture

An attempt to anticipate the future and project trends is essential for the survival of corporations. Towns and cities must project their population growths, population distributions, and their economic growth. Colleges and universities must always be planning ten or more years in advance. Recent studies in ecology project the terrible disasters that await mankind if it does not change its present practices of pollution.

It is just as mandatory for evangelicals to anticipate the future. They must project what they expect to be in order that they will be prepared for it. For evangelicalism to be strong and viable in the future, it must engage in projection and see what policies should be commenced now. This is the burden of this chapter.

Our Lord said that the gates of hell would not prevail against the church (Matt. 16:18). Whatever the expression *gates of hell* means, it means that the church will be subjected to a maximum force seeking to destroy, such as Satan or death. But our Lord promised that the church would survive this maximum oppression. Calvin stated this thesis eloquently:

> Even if the whole fabric of the world were overthrown, the church would neither totter nor fall. First, it stands by God's election, and cannot waver or fail any more than his eternal providence can. Secondly, it has in a way been joined to the steadfastness of Christ, who

will no more allow his believers to be estranged from him than that his members be rent and torn asunder.[1]

The evangelical believes that there will always be an evangelical church even though, again in the words of Calvin, it be "a small and contemptible number . . . hidden in a huge multitude and a few grains of wheat . . . covered by a pile of chaff." [2]

To prepare for the future the evangelical must be a real student of Holy Scripture. To be truly biblical is one of the most difficult achievements. We are always under pressures to see the Scriptures in other than their true meaning. We are always tempted to read our side of a theological debate into Scripture. There is always a movement that insists that some recent philosophy is the real speculative counterpart to the biblical revelation. Political and economic ideologies are not hesitant in looking to Scripture for additional support of their arguments. As children of our culture it is difficult to keep our culture from getting into our understanding of the meaning of Scripture. Because each person is the sum of his experiences, he cannot help but read Scripture through the lens of his personal history. There are always pressure groups pushing for relevancy or modernity, and the Scripture must fit their program.

To be biblical means to be relevant! But it means to be relevant the biblical way. The flow of thought must always be from the Scripture to the present situation. The reactionary who wants to understand his Bible in terms of the literature of a half a century or a century ago is not biblically relevant. If Holy Scripture is for every age, it is for this age and the next age. If we ossify and petrify our understanding of Scripture, it ceases to be the ever-living and therefore ever-relevant Word of God. We err if we put relevancy before Scripture; we also err if we hold onto Scripture in such a way we are irrelevant to our culture. That is why I believe that to be truly biblical is a rare and difficult achievement.

The first reason the evangelical must be thoroughly biblical is that until he is shown otherwise the one unique document of revelation is Holy Scripture, and this presents him with his most important and authoritative theological source. He cannot be a seed-picker (Acts 17:18—*spermologos*). The word *seed-picker* is a word of contempt. It depicts a bird that skips around the public square picking up the odd little bits of food he finds here and there. By extension it means any person who has an intellectual desire to learn but rather than being a deep thinker or a profound reflector picks up philosophical ideas from the marketplace without any sense of their coherence or depth of meaning. So much theological writing today is nothing more than seed-picking. Evangelicals too can be seed-pickers, but this is the sorriest kind of evangelical.

In order to master the contents of Holy Scripture as the definitive document of divine revelation in his theology, the evangelical must use the best possible sources and materials. That many of these materials are produced by nonevangelicals and that many of them are shaped by nonevangelical assumptions should not negate their use. The evangelical can settle for no less than the best possible resource materials, for at stake is the meaning of the highest possible document—Holy Scripture as God's revealed Word.

The second reason why evangelicals must be thorough in their knowledge of Scripture is that the theological world is a world of many options. Certainly many of these options are bewitching. Paul used a strong word in writing to the Galatians: *baskainō*, "to bewitch some one" (3:1). Theologians and philosophers are not only scholars but bewitchers, and it is easy for seminarians and pastors to be theologically bewitched. Theology is not only written as drab prose, but it can be written in a very clever manner. Evangelicals can be bewitched as others. How do evangelicals attempt to prevent theological bewitchment?

A lesson can be learned here from Barth. When the Nazis no longer permitted him to lecture at the University of Bonn, he left the lecture room by saying, "Exegesis, exegesis, exegesis!" What he meant was that the German nation was being bewitched by a special brew of Nazi ideology and Christian theology. Many times in his earlier years Hitler would stand before an audience with a Bible open in his hands, claiming that he was saying nothing more than what was in the Bible which the audience had learned at their mothers' knees. If the German Christians were to unmask this bewitching Nazi religion, it could only be done by continuous study of Holy Scripture. That was the meaning of his crying, "Exegesis, exegesis, exegesis!"

And so it is. If evangelicals are to remain true to their heritage, they cannot be seed-pickers in the theological market or easy victims of theological spellbinders. Only as evangelicals are deeply steeped in Scripture can they prevent themselves from being the victims of some new bewitching version of theology.

Theology may become a game of chess with the various theologians as the men on the board. Or, it may become "upmanship"—being superficially acquainted with a great number of theologians, books, and terms which a person skillfully uses in a theological conversation or in a bit of theological writing. Or, it can become a game where one pits one theologian against another and picks and chooses among the alternatives.

Evangelicals can be caught in these theological games as well as anybody else. However, my contention is that the basis for the theology of any evangelical must be a solid, substantial, and detailed knowledge of Holy Scripture. Only as he has this basis can he sort out and evaluate theologians, theologies, and theological concepts.

To the evangelical, theology is a matter of life and death, vindication or judgment, to be in the love of God or under the wrath of God. Theology must then be built on the most absolute foundation possible—the revelation of God in Scripture. And that revelation can only be known by the evangelical's becoming an expert in the exegesis of Scripture and a master of its contents. It has been said that both Luther and Calvin virtually knew the contents of the Bible by heart. Modern evangelicals ought to have the same such grasp of Holy Scripture. To an evangelical a decision for a theology is not like a choice among philosophies. In the latter it is a matter of intellectual persuasion or personal taste; in the former it is the way of life or the way of death.

Section 31: Evangelicals must know the inner structure of evangelical theology

That there are millions of evangelicals in America and the world was established by the statistics reported in the first chapter. How many of these evangelicals really understand evangelical theology is another matter. But if evangelicalism and evangelical theology are to remain strong options in the world of church and theology, evangelicals must become more articulate about the structure of evangelical theology.

When evangelicals really do not understand the structure of their theology, certain recognizable symptoms appear. It has been said that cults major on the minors. This is exactly what happens when evangelicals do not grasp in depth the meaning of their theology.

One of the most typical instances of majoring on the minors that reveals the loss of a real comprehension of evangelical theology is the undue attention given to eschatology or to odd views of eschatology. Eschatology with its emphasis on the future has a built-in existential appeal to it. It is therefore easy for evangelicals to get excited about eschatology. But either pathetically or tragically this eschatological emphasis is more cultic than biblical.

This can be verified by any Christian who will take the trouble to do it. First, such a person should study cults and sects that emphasize eschatology. After saturating himself with that literature, let him then read a lot of pop evangelical prophetic literature. The parallelisms are shocking.

When a cultic mentality is so apparent in evangelical literature, it is also apparent that many evangelicals have lost the sense of the inner structure of evangelical theology. Although this cultic element is easiest to detect in eschatology, it can manifest itself in other ways in the theological life of evangelicals. Whenever a secondary theological concern is made primary, a cultic mentality is at work. There is only one real method of preventing this, and that is for evangelicals to know their theology so well that they will not be led down cultic byways.

For example, when Abraham Kuyper was converted back to the orthodoxy of his home, he took five years to master Calvin. I would not equate the truth with Calvin or evangelical theology with Calvin, but this example illustrates the seriousness with which Kuyper took his theological conversion and the necessity of knowing its original formulation in minute detail. Perhaps today some student or pastor needs to give five hard years of labor to reading through his New Testament with great care. Or, perhaps he should read through the better volumes of *The Library of Christian Classics* or the more important monographs in the series, *Studies in Biblical Theology*.

There is the question of the staying power of theological literature. Some book may be exceedingly popular as of the present moment. For example, the sales of *Honest to God* and *Situation Ethics* were record breaking. But do these books have staying power? Will they be read seriously fifty years from now? Should a theological student spend his time with current best sellers? Or, should he appear outdated and out of step and study some book written fifty or more years ago which still maintains itself by its intrinsic merit like James Denney's *The Death of Christ?* Much recent interpretation of the atonement is so much theological trash when compared with Denney's careful scholarship. Certainly one's theological peers can intimidate him and make him feel that he is not with it if he isn't reading the latest theological best seller. But if an evangelical wishes to retain the integrity of his tradition, he should not be so intimidated.

There is another danger besides becoming an easy victim to the cultic when the evangelical fails to make himself really educated in his tradition, and that is that he has no real powers to assess contemporary theologians. For example, how can an evangelical who has specialized on the rapture and the millennium assess the merits and demerits of a theologian like Tillich or Bultmann or Moltmann? How can he really know if Moltmann's eschatology is biblical eschatology or a Christianized version of Bloch's Marxist revisionism?

Furthermore, if evangelical theology is to maintain itself as an option, it must be presented in sound academic form. It is unrealistic to think that if evangelical theology is stated from the perspective of profound theological scholarship it will be immediately accepted. G. C. Berkouwer's *Studies in Dogmatics* is just that, and while he is getting wide acceptance, he is not getting universal acceptance. If evangelical theology is to be criticized, it must be from basic principles and not from the standpoint of badly written, academically substandard evangelical works. Evangelical theology cannot escape either criticism or rejection, but it can be a more viable option if it is presented in the best academic tradition.

Section 32: Evangelicals must know their cultural climate

Kenneth Clark's *Civilization* makes such delightful reading because he shows so expertly the correlations between history and art. The same correlation of history and theology holds for theological science. To some degree theology is shaped by its age; theology also helps shape an age. Therefore, an evangelical theologian who wishes to know his theology in depth must study the correlations of theology and cultural history.

A good contemporary example of theology and cultural analysis is the writing of Thomas Torrance (*Theological Science; Space, Time, and Incarnation*; and *God and Rationality*). Torrance moves quite freely and competently back and forth from theology to science or from theology to philosophy or from theology to culture. Although he is not as close to the line of orthodox theology as Torrance, Helmut Thielicke is another very excellent example of a theologian who can move back and forth from culture to theology and theology to culture while maintaining the integrity of the Christian message. This cannot be said of some of our cultural theologians in America. They seem to have become so fascinated with cultural analysis and charting the drift of culture and society that they have lost the chart of divine revelation and have sacrificed theology to sociology.

Examples in the history of theology illustrating how the cultural climate influences theology are not difficult to find.

(1) Kant virtually reduced religion to ethics. The impact of this reduction on subsequent Protestant theology has been enormous. This becomes most apparent in the resolutions that national conventions pass. They are almost 100 percent concerned with social or economic or political affirmations, not theological ones. *The Theological Declaration of Barmen* (1934) is a happy exception.

(2) The Enlightenment sentimentalized the idea of God so that the wrath of God is understood as divine petulance. Ever since then the bulk of theologians have attempted to show that the wrath of God is either the consequences of our sins (for example, the alcoholic hangover is the divine wrath manifesting itself against the excessive use of alcohol) or the stern, disciplinary side of God's love (for example, the father spanks the child not to drain off his anger but in love to prevent the child from getting into further mischief which might endanger his life).

(3) Ethicists in modern times have insisted that sin and guilt are personal and unsharable. It is ethically impossible for one man to assume the guilt and penalty of another. This has resulted in a radical reevaluation of the atonement. Christ can no longer be our substitute and die our death because this is contrary to our understanding of ethical relationships. Hence, his death and atonement must be reconstructed on other lines such as a pure manifestation of love, or Christ enduring what any sinner would endure only with unwavering faith in God as he identifies himself with the human lot, or Christ being assaulted by the full force of the demonic on the cross yet resisting it successfully until death.

Unfortunately in the interpretation of the specific texts the real hard work of exegesis is bypassed, and the philosophical or theological assumptions ride rough-shod over the text. The forensic texts of the atonement suggesting some kind of vicarious or penal atonement are ignored or their importance completely underestimated. For example, there is no conceivable way that 2 Corinthians 5:21 ("For our sake he [God] made him [Christ] to be sin who knew no sin, that in him [Christ] we might become the righteousness of God," RSV) can be fitted into Aulén's theory of the atonement as a power struggle (*Christus Victor*), but this does not alter Aulén's interpretation.

Unless the point is lost we make it again: The impress of the cultural climate can be so strong that in the writing of theology certain concepts are eliminated, or diluted beyond their biblical meaning, or specific texts are not allowed to speak for themselves.

There is another virtue in knowing one's culture. Art is one of the clues to the mentality of an epoch. In his book *Civilization* Clark thinks that architecture is the best index of the character of a civilization. H. R. Rookmaaker (*Modern Art and the Death of a Culture*) believes that painting is most revelatory of the mood of a culture. It would not be amiss to say that Nathan Scott believes that literature is the clue to the pulse beat of culture. Others think that the status of poetry is the surest index of the health or sickness of a culture (for example, T. S. Eliot). Novels, plays, movies, and television programs are other modes through which a culture betrays its nature. Evangelicals, like Francis Schaeffer and Stuart Babbage (especially in literature), are making serious attempts to assess modern culture and its influence on theology.

There are certain dangers for the evangelical if he ignores cultural analysis and criticism: (1) A pastor may tend to foster a ghetto piety. He may so concentrate on his version of spirituality that the congregation—as well as himself—will become spiritually introverted. In such a state it is very difficult to communicate the Christian faith to one's contemporaries. To understand art and culture is not necessarily to approve of them, but it is necessary to understand them for purposes of evangelism and communication of the Christian faith.

(2) The other danger is that such a confined view of life will alienate people who do have a sense of culture, art, and literature. It may particularly alienate the young people who are being exposed to cultural history and literature in their education. The pastor and the theologian cannot be Philistines! A Philistine is a person who has no regard for or appreciation of culture. He differs from the barbarian who deliberately goes out of his way to destroy culture. To the contrary the Philistine ignores culture and art because he has centered all of his values and interests in his business or professional or occupational or recreational pursuits.

The God of Holy Scripture is a God of glory. One of the elements in the definition of glory is beauty. The glory of God is the external shining forth of the internal perfection and beauty of God. Not too much attention is given to the concept of God as a God of beauty in Scripture because there is an apparent fear that the aesthetic (or beautiful) will become an end itself and detract our attention from God. But even though it is a secondary motif, it is a biblical motif. Unfortunately it seldom is discussed in Christian theology. To our knowledge only Augustine and Barth have given the subject extensive treatment. If we are to worship God according to the fullness of his self-disclosure, we must also worship him as a God who is beautiful.

The evangelical concern with art and literature does have its function in helping the evangelical to understand his culture and therefore to communicate more effectively with it. But these concerns should also be part of his life in order that he be the full and complete man God intended in creation. The complete man is not only the spiritual man and the churchly man, he is also the man whose sense of the beautiful and the sublime have come to life.

The evangelical theologian should know the philosophies of his times. Whenever one reads a theologian, he must also look for the philosopher. Every theologian is to some measure also a philosopher. The basis of this assertion is that theology done in the proper way is interpretation, and interpretation involves assumptions, categories, criteria, concepts, forms of logic, and so on. These materials are derived from philosophy. It is imperative then for the evangelical to know his philosophies, for that is the necessary presupposition for his knowing and understanding his contemporary theologians.

The evangelical theologian and the evangelical pastor are not only spiritual pastors but pastors of the mind. They must counsel not only about personal problems but about theological opinions. They also may function in the larger context of their denomination where theological awareness is a primary requirement if the responsibility is to be discharged with highest fidelity. Only as a pastor understands the theological options of the times can he function as a theological counselor or advisor. And he can understand the theological options only if he has some understanding of the philosophical options of the times.

If a student comes to his pastor and asks him about some difficulty with his theological beliefs and the pastor cuts him off with a "let us pray about this," the pastor has lost the student. A burning theological problem requires a responsible response! We do not rule out prayer, but prayer is not to be used as a means to evade a painful question. The same is true in theological education. An evangelical professor cannot handle modern theology by the simple expedient of writing it all off to unbelief. The student has a right to receive from his evangelical professor a reliable evaluation of modern theologies, theologians, and theological issues. The devil does have his "flaming darts" of unbelief (Eph. 6:16) which are to be intercepted by the shield of faith. But the student will be wary of a professor's shield of faith if he has shielded himself from the contemporary theological scene.

To stay in the theological conversation at the level of the church, denomination, college, or seminary, the evangelical has to interact with the theology of his times, and he can only do that as he is to some responsible measure acquainted with the philosophies of his times.

It is true that Paul says that the wisdom of this world does not know God (1 Cor. 1:21); that the natural man with all his philosophy cannot understand spiritual things (1 Cor. 2:14); and that philosophy can lead us astray from Christ (Col. 2:8). But this does not mean that evangelicals should abstain from philosophy as some have argued. It means that the evangelical must be aware of the right way for a Christian to interact with philosophers and philosophies.

The evangelical ought to have some comprehension of the science of his times. There are always popular books that the layman can read in order to learn the latest theories in science, so a pastor does not have to be a scientist to have some awareness of the character of modern science. The evangelical should know that there are some major differences about the nature of scientific knowledge itself. There is some difference between Hans Reichenbach (*The Rise of Scientific Philosophy*) and Michael Polányi (*Personal Knowledge*). Much pro and con has been written on Thomas Kuhn's famous book, *The Structure of Scientific Revolutions* (1962). How much subjectivity there is in scientific theory is analyzed in Israel Shefler's *Science and Subjectivity* (1967).

Unfortunately, as we have noted, the Bible-science controversy has not subsided among evangelicals and fundamentalists. The pastor with some insight into science can protect his congregation from those views that are extremely obscurantistic and reactionary.

In a sense there is a deeper problem facing the evangelical of both the present and the future than the Bible-science one. How does an evangelical live in a technological society? The city of the future is called the technopolis. How does an evangelical live in technopolis? What so many contemporary evangelicals do not realize is that living in technopolis means a new consciousness, a new frame of reference, a new way of looking at problems. The man who struggled so hard with this problem because he saw it in depth perhaps more than any other theologian was Dietrich Bonhoeffer. He is both difficult to understand and systematically misinterpreted because theologians and evangelicals do not know the problems to which he was speaking.

With technopolis comes not only a whole battery of scientific miracles and sophisticated gadgets utterly beyond our imagination, but a whole new consciousness. Bonhoeffer's question was: What is the Christian version of this new consciousness? What does the supernatural mean in a science of man-made miracles? What does prayer mean in a society where technology answers prayers? What does faith mean when sight can solve so many problems? This is the foreboding crisis for the evangelical as the world of increasing technological sophistication settles down upon him and the Christian church.

Evangelicals must be students of psychology. Just as science through technology is answering our prayers, so to speak, psychology seems to be replacing the Holy Spirit. Behavioral changes which we have usually turned over to the power of the Spirit are now being made by psychological methods. Spiritual problems are now psychological problems. The idea of praying through so current in nineteenth-century Christian piety is replaced by counseling or therapy groups.

Is it a case of either/or? Is it the Spirit or psychology or is it the Spirit and psychology? Is praying through still part of the way evangelicals solve their personal problems as well as by counseling? Evangelicals need to know of these tensions. Much hard thinking yet needs to be done on the correlation of psychology and Christian piety. The writings of Paul Tournier are deceiving in the sense that he writes so simply and directly. Christians with no psychological background can read him with profit. Yet underneath his simple paragraphs is a profound knowledge of modern theory in psychiatry. If an evangelical will read Tournier shrewdly enough and really read between the lines, he will find some of the best correlation done today between a robust Christian theology and a very professional and expert knowledge of psychology. But this burden should not rest upon one man. We need more evangelicals of the same order as Tournier—thoroughly knowledgeable in theology and expert in psychiatry—to make the correlations necessary in the increasing world of psychological sophistication of Christian spirituality and psychotherapeutical methods.

The current expression *keep in touch* means that distance separates friends and that separation by distance can become separation of fellowship by default. And so it is that with the cultural surrounding of the evangelical and the elements within that culture the evangelical ought to keep in touch. We use this expression very intentionally. We have no unrealistic ideal that every evangelical pastor and evangelical theologian should have a mastery of all the developments within a culture. But evangelical pastors and educators should keep in touch with culture. If there is a big shift in philosophical thought, they should know about it. If the sociologists have noticed a marked change in a given trend, the evangelical should know of that change. If educational theory undergoes radical reconstruction, evangelicals should know that too. The simple observation I am making is that evangelicals ought not to wake up ten to twenty years after such major cultural shifts have taken place. They ought to keep in touch even though they might not be able to understand the new movements with the depth they would wish.

Section 33: Evangelicals must be diligent students of linguistics, philosophy of language, and communications

Here we have three overlapping disciplines that are in the process of rapid change and development. The evangelical has two concerns with these disciplines: (i) Holy Scripture is a product of all three: It is a linguistic phenomenon; it reflects a certain philosophy of language; and it was produced for communication. (ii) The evangelical of today is evangelistically minded and to be able to preach the gospel—using the word *preach* very flexibly—to his generation he must know something of these three overlapping disciplines.

My first concern is with how the theories of revelation and inspiration must be restated. Historically the problems of language, inspiration, and revelation have been approached by theologians exclusively trained in traditional theories of language and with years and years of study especially in Greek and Latin. Perhaps one should not overlook either the conscious or unconscious importation into langauge of Aristotelian logic. Out of this nexus the classical doctrines of inspiration and revelation were formulated.

However, modern studies of linguistics inspired by the growth of modern anthropology, modern studies in the philosophy of language, modern philosophical developments in linguistic philosophy, and modern development of communications theory calls for a rethinking by evangelicals of the twin doctrines of revelation and inspiration. Certainly communications theory is the more natural habitat of Holy Scripture than a scientific textbook on comparative philology.

This does not mean that the older theories were totally wrong. Communications theory and linguistic studies do not eliminate grammar, but they relocate it in a larger context. Furthermore, any new theory in the science of learning incorporates within itself whatever is of value of the older theory. Much of what previous theologians have said of inspiration and revelation is still relevant.

The last great impetus to rethink revelation came from the neoorthodox. Neoorthodox theologians believed that liberalism had so recast the doctrine of revelation that there was no means of discerning what was the voice of man and what was the voice of God. When revelation was reduced to insight or intuition or moral perception, then the boundary between the human word and the divine Word was lost. The neoorthodox theologians attempted to restate the doctrine of revelation to correct this. The Word of God was given such a uniqueness of origin and mystery of content that it could not be confused with the voice of man. Regardless of whether or not some evangelicals agree with Barth or Brunner or Weber or Torrance, these men are one with the evangelicals in affirming against the liberal theologians that there is a real difference between the word of man and the Word of God.

It is my conviction that the next impetus to rethink our evangelical doctrines of inspiration and revelation is going to come from the modern communications theory.

One of the few ventures of evangelicals into this field is an essay by Terry Martin. Although he is reacting particularly with McLuhan, what he has to say spills over into the communications theory in general.[3] His point is that the communications theory is changing our entire concept of the process of communication, and the Christian and Holy Scripture are caught in the midst of this change and ferment. He makes the same point that I have made above, that if

Christians are really to stay in conversation with future developments
in speech, linguistics, communications, and philosophy of language,
they must be able to restate their beliefs in inspiration and revelation
in these contexts.

A critical example is the concept of myth. Unfortunately the concept of myth has been given a bad name in theology by Strauss (*Life
of Christ,* 1835–36) and in modern times by Rudolph Bultmann.
Some evangelical circles are so up tight about myth that even to
breathe the word with some positive affirmation is to invite a charge
of terrible heresy. Gustaf Aulén in his latest work, *The Drama and
the Symbols,* feels that Bultmann has done theology a terrible dis-
service by giving myth such an odious interpretation. All the richness
of the biblical revelation about God, claims Aulén, is in mythical,
symbolical, and metaphorical language, and for Bultmann to so
prejudice the concept of myth as utterly reprehensible to modern man
is literally to mess up our whole process of understanding the biblical
revelation of God.

But supposing we relocate myth, redefine it, and see its function
differently? Under such conditions can there be a positive evangelical
version of myth? Naturally if an evangelical persists in seeing myth as
Strauss, Bultmann, and other critics have seen it, then he will not
tolerate such a possibility. But if myth can be seen in a newer context, perhaps there is a sense in which evangelicals may use the concept. If myth is one of the major counters in the communications
theory, it may have a place in evangelical theology.

Let us look at some of the possibilities. Brunner and Niebuhr use
myth in a good sense. It is the essential character of theological
language. Theological language differs from ordinary language in that
it is a mixed language. It speaks at the same time of things earthly
and heavenly, of things worldly and spiritual, of things visible and
invisible. Theology cannot escape such mixed language. If this is the
case, then an evangelical need have no real objection to myth in this
context.

Or, we may look into Paul Ricoeur's *The Symbolism of Evil.* To
him the myth is the only way the universal and transhistorical character of religious experience can be expressed. It is therefore an acceptable genre of communications. Again in this sense the evangelical
need not in principle reject Ricoeur's definition of myth. F. W. Dillistone has edited a book, *Myth and Symbol,*[4] in which different
writers attempt to show the positive function of myth in theological

discourse differing radically from Bultmann's concept of myth. For example, the essay by Eliade, "Myths, Dreams, and Mysteries," shows the positive function of myth in man's religions in contrast to the very negative assessment of myth by modern rationalistic and positivistic thinkers (such as Bultmann and the new hermeneutic). The Roman Catholic writer, Aidan M. Carr, has written a short article, "Myth Revisited," to argue in much the same way as Eliade, namely, although myth has been given a bad name in recent theology by such men as Bultmann, there is a positive, constructive, biblical, and Christian use of myth.[5]

To repeat: To evangelicals the word *myth* is bad. But what if further studies in communications show that myth is one of the valid methods of representing truth and particularly religious truth? Do we then stubbornly stick with the debate about myth frozen around Bultmann, or will we have the flexibility to see myth in the new light in which modern linguistics, communications, and the study of comparative religion see it and find a place for it in evangelical theology?

Myths in Holy Scripture presented no offense to such evangelical literary geniuses as C. S. Lewis and T. S. Eliot, for in their specialty myth is one of the higher forms of literary communication and therefore any mythical elements in Scripture did not offend them but even enhanced the power of Scripture to communicate. Lewis accused Bultmann of having a very defective and therefore irrelevant view of mythology.

Furthermore, so much is happening in linguistics and language theory that the evangelical must know something of this as he rethinks his doctrines of inspiration and revelation. As has already been indicated, theologians work from the stance of classical philology. However, modern linguistics has shown the fallacy of so many assumptions of classical philology. The evangelical who is with it should be working from the science of modern linguistics and not from the untrustworthy theories of classical linguistics.

New theories of the nature of language and how it is learned by a child are being developed. The most famous name in this regard is Chomsky. Others are working with an existential theory of language which stems eventually from Heidegger but is related to theological language and preaching. The best example of this is the new hermeneutic. Still another view of language comes from linguistic or analytic philosophy. Its concern is with the nature of theological language based upon philosophical investigations of language. The

most impressive name among the philosophers in this movement is
that of Ludwig Wittgenstein.[6] I have already mentioned the strong
influence of McLuhan on the problem of communication.[7]

I mention these movements in linguistics, philosophy, and theory
of communications to reinforce the thesis: In order to understand
the process of revelation and the character of inspiration and thereby
be in a position to restate both concepts in the light of modern developments, evangelicals must come to terms with modern linguistics,
modern theories of communication, and contemporary linguistic or
analytic philosophy.[8]

But the complication does not end here! Archeologists, historians,
and scholars in the field of literature are turning to the computer to
help solve problems. Just as a machine is an extension of the power
of the human arm and hand, the computer is the extension of the
power of the human mind. A computer can work with the speed of
electrical current; it can retain thousands of items a human mind
cannot; and it can discover correlations that are either impossible for
the human mind to discover or that would take the human mind an
incredibly long time to discover.

Already the computer is being used by literary historians. Initial
attempts have been made to use it to solve problems of biblical criticism. At the present time there is resistance by evangelicals to the use
of computers in biblical criticism on the basis that they cannot really
sort out certain intangible factors. But let us project into the future.
Computers are going to become more and more sophisticated. The
amount of material that can be fed into them will greatly increase. The
criteria of selection or classification will also increase. It could well be
that biblical criticism will be done almost totally with computers in
the future. Even matters of change in style, great variations in subject matter, or the difference between the style of a man when he
was young and when he was elderly will be properly sorted out and
assessed by computers.

If this is the case—and we predict that it will be—evangelicals
must be prepared for what is now being called "future shock." Evangelicals will be forced to rethink the entire problem of the authenticity
of Scripture (the power of Scripture as a written document to function as the Word of God). Evangelicals who do not anticipate what
computers will solve in the future with reference to all the literary
documents of antiquity are very nearsighted. They need to be doing

some pioneering ("proleptic") thinking now on the possible solutions to the new problems.

Section 34: Evangelicals must rethink the manner in which God is related to the world

When Bishop Robinson published his work, *Honest to God,* he made the problem of how we are to think of God's relationship to his world and man an international theological problem. He rejected the ideas of "God up there" and "God out there" for Tillich's idea of "God in here." Robinson was not the first modern theologian to wrestle with this problem or the last. Nor is he the one that did the best job with it. His fame rests in bringing it so frankly and, one could say, brutally to the surface.

God's immanence and transcendence have been discussed for centuries. If Calvinists were accused of overemphasizing the transcendence of God, religious liberals were accused of virtually eliminating it to defend the immanence of God. This they expressed in the word *panentheism* ("God is in all things"—a definition of the immanence of God, short of pantheism). Barth, Brunner, and Bultmann have been accused of overcompensating for the immanence of God as taught in liberalism with too strong a doctrine of divine transcendence. Others have accused Tillich of being a pantheist with his concept of God as the Ground of all Being.

Part of the problem is that transcendence and immanence are essentially spatial terms, and modern astronomy has so radically changed our understanding of space that our ideas of transcendence and immanence have become ambiguous. The other part of the problem is the emphasis on the God-to-man relationship as being existential, which must be stated in personal categories. How is transcendence and immanence to be restated in personal or existential terms?

One of the recent efforts to combine a modern scientific understanding of space and existential space is that of the German scientist turned theologian, Karl Heim. Heim thought that the entire modern Christian apologetic turned on a reformulation of a theory of space, correlating it with scientific space, God's transcendence, God's immanence, and existential space. Barth attempted to modify the extreme doctrine of transcendence in his *Epistle to the Romans* with a small book on *The Humanity of God,* wherein the doctrine of the incarnation balances the transcendence of God of his earlier writings.

Some recent theological literature attempts to solve the problem in terms of dimensional thinking. God's action in the world is not to be pictured as hovering over the earth as the stage of the divine action, but as God's action in the world as one of the many other dimensions within the world. By so thinking, it is believed that the problems of the older supernaturalism are relieved, and yet the uniqueness of God's work in the world is not lost. Peter Berger's *A Rumor of Angels* seeks to find the transcendental in many facets of man's social life—not like a clap of thunder but more like the rustle of feathers. In his work, *Religion and the Scientific Future,* Langdon Gilkey locates the assumptions in the scientific method which of themselves are not established by science. He calls this the mythology of science, and says that they too are perhaps "rumors of angels."

The theologians of hope or of futurology restate the transcendence of God in terms of God's being the pull or the lure of the future. Here is the combination of both a spatial and a temporal element. God is pictured as spatially out in front of history pulling history in his direction and temporally as the God of the future out there ahead of history in anticipation of where history ought to be going and therefore the clue for what man is to be doing. Modern process theology comes close to modern theology of hope in thinking of the relationship of God to the world, at least in the sense of God being the God of the future. The process theologians have a more complex metaphysical or philosophical manner in which they relate God to the world and man, but they stress the divine immanence and the divine as the dimensional in character and not transcendental in a traditional orthodox sense.

This is not an exhaustive list but a suggestive list representing different ways men are rethinking God's relationship to the world and rethinking the doctrine of the divine transcendence. The question for the evangelical of the future is that having thought through the biblical doctrine of creation, God's relationship to man, divine immanence and transcendence as taught in Scripture, how can he reformulate the biblical witness in light of modern philosophy, modern science, and modern theology? Are there models other than the traditional ones which he may better employ to present his theology? This does not mean a capitulation to modern mentality which is the disease which infects most contemporary theology, but rather a restatement or reformulation or reconceptualization of the biblical message about

God, the world, and transcendence, which does not surrender the uniqueness of the scriptural revelation and at the same time remains in real communication with his own generation.

Apparently there is a very high degree of dissatisfaction all the way around among reflective theologians about God's relationship to the world and the problem of transcendence.[9] This is not a trivial discussion, and evangelical theologians of the future must interact with it in a responsible manner. Perhaps we shall find in the final analysis that what Luther [10] or Calvin [11] had to say comes closest to the matter. Or, perhaps some of the newer conceptualizing will be found digestible to evangelical theology. It might be that the crux of the matter rests in a radical approach to the doctrine of creation or a new formulation of the doctrine of the Holy Spirit. It is not my intention to give an interpretation now or suggest the way in which the interpretation will be reached. My concern is that evangelical theologians be concerned.

In summary these are some of the things that evangelicals of the future must be wrestling with if evangelical theology is going to remain a viable option for generations yet unborn. We believe that the gates of hell shall not prevail against the church. A similar truth is stated in Malachi 3:6 wherein it is claimed that Israel is preserved in spite of her sinfulness because "I the Lord do not change; therefore you, O sons of Jacob, are not consumed" (that is, do not cease to exist).

The evangelical agrees with Calvin on the indefectability of the invisible church which will in turn always have a representative body of men on earth (in contrast to the Roman Catholic version of indefectability as the indefectability of the Roman Catholic church).[12] He is therefore basically optimistic: God's purposes in the church and for the church will not fail (even though the count of true witnesses recognized on the earth may get down to one—Elijah, 1 Kings 19:10).

But the evangelical of the present and the future also realizes that what he does and how he witnesses is part of the divine plan for the indefectability of the church. And therefore a counterpart to the divine faithfulness must be the evangelical's promotion of his faith with rigor and vigor. He must keep sensitive, open, and informed to all the changes going on around him, and being harmless as a dove but wise as a serpent learn how he can ever keep evangelical theology informed by the best of modern learning, defended by the soundest of arguments screened by centuries of progress in the sciences and in logic, and propagated by all the methods modern technology and modern educational theory can provide him. If these things are done, there is a great and exciting future for evangelical theology. If we fail, we shall be the church of lost causes, the church of skirmishes and not battles, and the church of the rear guard and not the avant garde.

NOTES

1. Calvin, *Institutes,* bk. 4, para. 1, fn. 3.
2. Ibid., bk. 4, para. 1, 2.
3. Terry Martin, "The Medium Is the Message," *Christian Graduate* (December 1970) 23:97–100. He lists five things we can learn from McLuhan (and I give them as a sample of what I have in mind concerning Christian interaction and the communications theory, not to canonize McLuhan). (1) We must see the relation of culture to communication and its relationship to our senses. (2) Differences in religions may be more in the media used to communicate than in the historic doctrines themselves. (3) Since the Bible is a medium of communication, we must rethink the Bible in this context, including McLuhan's idea of myth. (4) We must become more openminded in our approval or disapproval of media (for example, movies). (5) We must be aware of the danger of losing Christian dogma in emphasis on communication.
4. F. W. Dillistone, ed., *Myth and Symbol* (Naperville, Ill.: Allenson, 1966).
5. Aidan M. Carr, "Myth Revisited," *American Ecclesiastical Review* (August 1970) 163:85–91.
6. A number of books survey the problems raised by linguistic philosophy and the possible theological replies. See W. T. Blackstone, *The Problem of Religious Knowledge* (Englewood Cliffs, N.J.: Prentice-Hall, 1963); Dallas High, ed., *New Essays on Religious Language* (New York: Oxford University Press, 1969); Ronald E. Santoni, ed., *Religious Language and the Problem of Religious Knowledge* (Bloomington, Ind.: Indiana University Press, 1968); Ian T. Ramsey, *Religious Language* (New York: Macmillan, 1963); Jerry Gill, *The Possibility of Religious Knowledge* (Grand Rapids, Mich.: Wm. B. Eerdmans, 1971).
7. See Gerald E. Stearn, ed., *McLuhan: Hot and Cool* (New York: New American Library, 1967); and R. Rosenthal, *McLuhan: Pro and Con* (New York: Funk and Wagnalls, 1968). McLuhan has also made an educational film in which he explains his theory.
8. Unfortunately, one of the conflicts that will inevitably arise within the evangelical camp will be between those evangelicals who understand the present sophistication of knowledge in linguistics, philosophy of language, and the communications theory and those evangelicals who

have no idea of this sophistication. I predict that the latter will accuse the former of using purely human means to decide divine truth.

9. See Martin Marty and Dean Peerman, eds., *New Theology No. 7: The Recovery of Transcendence* (New York: Macmillan, 1970). Bonhoeffer's thought about man come of age and not using God as a crutch or to fill the gaps is approaching the issue from another direction. See also William Pollard, *Chance and Providence: God's Action in a World Governed by Scientific Law* (New York: Charles Scribner's Sons, 1958).

10. See Hans Schwarz, "Luther's Understanding of Heaven and Hell: Theology or Cosmology," *Interpreting Luther's Legacy*, ed. F. W. Meuser and S. D. Schneider (Philadelphia: Augsburg, 1969), pp. 83–94.

11. Compare Cole, "The Secret Providence of God," *Calvin's Calvinism*, and the *Institutes*, bk. 1, chaps. 16–18. Although Calvin has been branded a theological determinist and Calvinism has been taken too deterministically, it has been called Islamic nevertheless. As unexpected as it may seem, Calvin's idea of the divine presence and action in the world is very close to concepts found in the new process theology. The concept of the divine presence and divine impingement on creation are very similar. Process theologians have the advantage of added information from modern science about the ups and downs of the evolutionary process and the concept of maneuverable contingency which is behind scientific experimentation.

12. I do not know if Hans Küng is aware of Calvin's doctrine of the indefectability of the church, but in his book, *Infallibility? An Inquiry*, Küng opts for Calvin's view of the indefectability of the church, which always lives under the promise of the truth of God in place of papal, conciliar, and biblical infallibility.

NAME INDEX

Alexander, 87
Anselm, 124
Arius, 15, 120
Athanasius, 15, 21, 57
Augustine, 15, 18, 30, 32, 57, 58, 96, 97, 124, 132, 159
Aulen, 158, 164

Babbage, S., 158
Barth, 21, 54, 70, 93, 104, 106, 107, 108, 109, 110, 114, 116, 118, 130, 143, 153, 163, 167
Ad Limina Apostolorum, 117
allegorical method, 115
Antwort, 30
as situation ethicist, 120
atonement, 119
attack on liberalism, 111 ff.
Christomonism versus Christo-
centrism, 119
criticism of Roman Catholic
theology, 116 ff.
critique of Schleiermacher, 76
evangelical use, 113
Gospel and Law, 44
on communism, 120
one covenant, 119
on glory, 159
Scripture, 146
wrath of God, 119
Benz, 20
Berger, P., 168
Berkouwer, G. C., 110, 156
The Person of Christ, 56
Bettenson, H., *Documents of the
Christian Church,* 50
Beza, *Tractationes Theologicae,* 45
Bicknell, E. J., *A Theological In-*

*troduction to the Thirty-nine
Articles,* 51
Biedermann, 79
Blamire, H., 144
Bloch, E., 147, 156
Boniface VIII, 23
Bousset, 97
Braun, F., 125
Bromiley, 110
Brunner, 104, 106, 107, 108, 111, 113, 114, 116, 118, 120, 130, 143, 146, 163, 164, 167
Bucer, 38
Bultmann, 70, 73, 85, 104, 107, 108, 149, 156, 164, 165, 167
Bushnell, H., 145

Calvin, 15, 26, 29, 30, 33, 34, 38, 43, 45, 52, 58, 93, 96, 115, 116, 124, 151 f., 154, 155, 169
Commentaries, 34
institutes, letters, tracts, com-
mentaries, 50
*Institutes of the Christian Reli-
gion,* 58
on reason, culture, etc., 133 ff.
Carpenter, 51
Carr, A., 165
Cauthen, K., 80
*The Impact of American Reli-
gious Liberalism,* 75
Channing, W., 80
Chillingworth, 59
Chomsky, 165
Clark, G., 110
Clark, K., 156, 158
Cocceius, J., 129

172

SUBJECT INDEX

flat view of, 126
interprets Scripture, 33
majesty of, 27
seats of doctrine, 114
Second Helvetic Confession, 51
see (*sedes*), 18
seed-picker, 152
Sentences, 30
separatism, 139
Septuagint, 27
sin and guilt, 157
Situation Ethics, 155
sobornost, 18
Social Gospel, 82, 84, 126, 127, 145
sola
  Christus, 144
  fide, 144
  gratia, 144
  Scriptura, 30, 59, 113, 144
son, 15
specialized evangelism, 89
Spirit, 15
  and Word, 34
  witness of, 33
Studies in Biblical Theology, 107, 155
Summa Theologica, 15, 18, 23, 30
supernatural
  rejected, 78
  suspect, 69
symbols, 125
System, The, 62

thematic clarity, 33
theological
  bewitchment, 153
  systems, 84
Theological Declaration of Barmen, 157
theology
  academic dignity of, 146
  of the cross, 62
  species of, 140 f.
Third Council of Toledo, 20
Thirty-nine Articles of Religion, 31, 45
toleration, religious, 66

Tower Experience, 35
tradition, 29 f., 128, 129
  oral, 25
Tradition, 15, 25, 29, 32
traditions, 15
transcendence, 167
translation of Bible into German, 28
transubstantiation, 18
Trinity, 57
truth and scriptural concern, 124 f.
TULIP, 46
Turks, 51
Twenty-five Articles of Religion, 46

Unam Sanctum, 23
Unitarianism, 79
United States News and World Report, 11
universalism, 82, 136
Urbild, 14, 82
utopia, 135

value statements, 95
Vatican I, 19
Vatican II, 26
Vincentian Canon, 13
visible words of God, 38
vowel points inspired, 60

Wartburg castle, 28
Westminster Confession, 51, 59
witness of the Spirit, 33, 60, 61, 131
Wittenberg, 34, 41
wooden-headed literalist, 125
Word
  and Act of God, 13
  and Spirit, 34, 60, 61
  behind the words, 125
  of God, 24, 25, 26, 27, 30, 33, 38, 83, 84, 112, 124
World Council of Churches, 88
world redefined, 83
World's Christian Fundamentals Association, 88
World War II, 105
wrath of God, 157

Bernard Ramm (1916–1992) served as professor of Christian theology at American Baptist Seminary of the West. During his lifetime he wrote more than fifteen books in areas such as apologetics, hermeneutics, theology, and ethics.